Agentic AI for Beginners

A Practical Guide to Understanding and Leveraging Autonomous Systems

Written By

Camila Jones

Copyright

Table of Contents

Chapter Introduction to Agentic AI

1.1 What Is Agentic AI?

Definition and Overview

Agentic AI refers to artificial intelligence systems that operate with a degree of autonomy or "agency." In simple terms, these are AI systems designed to make decisions, take actions, and pursue specific goals without constant human intervention. Unlike traditional AI models that only perform tasks when explicitly commanded, agentic AI possesses the ability to plan, learn from its environment, and act independently to achieve desired outcomes.

Key Characteristics

To better understand Agentic AI, consider the following core **characteristics:**

Characteristic	Description
Autonomy	**The ability to operate independently by making decisions based on internal goals and external inputs.**
Adaptability	The capacity to learn and adjust its behavior over time, using techniques like reinforcement learning and feedback loops.
Goal-Oriented Behavior	Designed to pursue specific objectives or tasks, often defined by developers or through machine learning processes.

Interaction with Environment	Ability to sense, interpret, and react to changes in its surroundings, whether physical or digital.
Decision-Making	Uses algorithms to analyze available data and decide on the best course of action, often simulating human-like reasoning processes.

This table summarizes the main attributes of agentic AI in an accessible way. Agentic AI blends aspects of traditional rule-based systems with modern machine learning, enabling it to perform tasks more dynamically and efficiently.

How Agentic AI Works

At its core, agentic AI involves several interconnected components:

- **Perception:** The system collects data from its environment using sensors or data inputs. This could be through cameras, microphones, or digital data streams.
- **Reasoning and Decision-Making:** Using algorithms—often based on machine learning or reinforcement learning—the AI interprets the data to decide on an action.
- **Action:** Once a decision is made, the AI acts autonomously to influence its environment. This might involve sending commands to other systems, moving a robot, or simply providing a recommendation.
- **Feedback Loop:** After taking an action, the system receives feedback from the environment. This feedback is then used to improve future decisions, making the system adaptive.

Simple Code Example: Simulated Autonomous Agent

Below is a simplified Python example that demonstrates the basic structure of an autonomous agent. This example uses a simulated environment where an agent attempts to reach a target location using basic decision-making.

```python
import random

class AutonomousAgent:
    def __init__(self, start_position, target_position):
        self.position = start_position
        self.target = target_position
        self.steps_taken = 0

    def perceive_environment(self):
        # For simplicity, the environment is the difference between current position and target.
        return self.target - self.position

    def decide_action(self, difference):
        # Decide to move closer to the target.
        # In a more complex system, this would involve advanced algorithms.
        if difference > 0:
            return 1  # Move right
        elif difference < 0:
            return -1  # Move left
        else:
            return 0  # Stay
```

```python
    def act(self, action):
        self.position += action
        self.steps_taken += 1

    def is_target_reached(self):
        return self.position == self.target

    def run(self):
        print(f"Starting at position {self.position}, aiming for {self.target}")
        while not self.is_target_reached():
            diff = self.perceive_environment()
            action = self.decide_action(diff)
            self.act(action)
            print(f"Step {self.steps_taken}: Moved {action}, new position is {self.position}")
        print("Target reached!")


# Example usage:
if __name__ == "__main__":
    agent = AutonomousAgent(start_position=0, target_position=10)
    agent.run()
```

Explanation of the Code:

- **Class Initialization:** The AutonomousAgent is initialized with a starting position and a target position.
- **Perception:** The method perceive_environment calculates the difference between the current position and the target, simulating the agent's sensing mechanism.
- **Decision-Making:** The decide_action method uses a simple rule: move right if the target is to the right, move left if to the left, or stay if already at the target.
- **Action:** The act method updates the position based on the decided action.
- **Loop Execution:** The run method continuously performs perception, decision-making, and action until the target is reached, printing each step.

This example, while simple, encapsulates the essence of agentic AI: autonomous decision-making based on perception and a feedback loop to adjust actions.

1.2. Why Agentic AI Matters Today

Relevance in Modern Technology

Agentic AI is becoming increasingly important as technology evolves. In today's fast-paced digital environment, many applications require systems that can act independently. For instance, autonomous vehicles, smart home devices, and digital assistants all rely on AI that can make real-time decisions without waiting for human input.

Enhancing Efficiency and Productivity

One of the major benefits of agentic AI is its ability to enhance productivity by automating repetitive or complex tasks. By taking on decision-making roles, these systems can:

- **Reduce Human Workload:** Automate routine processes in manufacturing, logistics, and even administrative tasks, freeing up human workers for more creative or complex responsibilities.
- **Improve Speed:** Execute tasks faster than human operators, especially in data-driven environments where rapid analysis and action are crucial.
- **Increase Accuracy:** With the right algorithms and training data, agentic AI can reduce errors and ensure consistent performance over time.

Driving Innovation

Agentic AI is a key driver of innovation in various sectors:

- **Healthcare:** Autonomous systems can assist in diagnostics, patient monitoring, and even surgical procedures, potentially improving outcomes and reducing human error.
- **Finance:** In algorithmic trading and fraud detection, agentic AI can analyze vast amounts of data in real time and make split-second decisions that might outperform human analysts.
- **Smart Cities:** Agentic AI can optimize traffic flow, manage energy consumption, and enhance public safety by integrating with sensors and infrastructure, leading to more efficient urban management.

Real-World Impact

To illustrate the significance of agentic AI, consider the following case study in table format:

Application Area	Example	Impact
Autonomous Vehicles	Self-driving cars (e.g., Tesla)	Improved road safety, reduced traffic congestion, and enhanced mobility for those unable to drive.
Healthcare	Robotic surgery and diagnostic tools	Faster diagnosis, precision in surgical procedures, and reduced hospital stay times for patients.
Finance	Algorithmic trading systems	Increased market efficiency, improved risk management, and the ability to process complex market data.

| **Smart Homes** | AI-powered assistants (e.g., Alexa) | Streamlined home management, energy savings, and improved quality of life through automation of daily tasks. |

Societal and Ethical Considerations

With the growing power of agentic AI comes a need to address ethical and social implications:

- **Accountability:** As systems become more autonomous, determining responsibility in case of failure becomes more complex.
- **Bias and Fairness:** Ensuring that AI systems make decisions free from bias is essential, particularly when these systems impact areas like employment, healthcare, or law enforcement.
- **Privacy:** With enhanced capabilities comes the need for robust data protection measures to ensure that personal information is not misused.

Summary

Agentic AI matters today because it represents a paradigm shift in how technology interacts with the world. By incorporating autonomy, adaptability, and decision-making capabilities, these systems are not only revolutionizing industries but also shaping the future of work, healthcare, finance, and beyond. As the technology matures, agentic AI has the potential to unlock significant efficiencies and drive innovation—making it a critical area of focus for businesses, researchers, and policymakers alike.

1.3. Who Should Read This Book?

This book is designed for a broad range of readers who are interested in the emerging field of agentic AI. Whether you are completely new to the concept or already have some experience with artificial intelligence, you will find valuable insights and practical guidance within these pages.

Target Audiences

Below is a table summarizing the primary groups that will benefit from this guide:

Audience	Description	What You Will Gain
Tech Professionals	Engineers, data scientists, and IT specialists seeking to understand and implement autonomous systems in their work.	Practical techniques, best practices, and technical insights.
Business Managers & Leaders	Executives and managers interested in integrating AI solutions into their organizations for improved decision-making and productivity.	Strategic case studies, ethical considerations, and real-world examples.
Students and Beginners	Individuals new to AI or those with a basic understanding who wish to build a strong foundation in agentic AI concepts and applications.	Step-by-step explanations, interactive exercises, and accessible language.
Entrepreneurs & Innovators	Start-up founders and innovators exploring new business opportunities enabled by autonomous systems.	Insights into disruptive innovations, market trends, and practical guides.

Why You Should Read This Book

- **Practical Learning:** The book is structured to deliver real-world examples and interactive elements that make learning engaging and applicable.
- **Balanced Content:** It bridges the gap between technical depth and accessible explanations so that both experts and newcomers can benefit.

- **Future-Proof Knowledge:** With emerging trends in agentic AI, this guide prepares you to understand and leverage autonomous systems as they continue to evolve.
- **Actionable Outcomes:** Each chapter provides clear learning outcomes and hands-on exercises that empower you to apply the concepts immediately in your work or studies.

1.4. How to Use This Guide (Including Learning Outcomes & Interactive Diagrams)

This guide is designed not just as a reading experience but as an interactive learning tool. It's organized to help you build your knowledge step by step, ensuring that each concept is fully understood before moving on to the next. Here's how to get the most out of it:

Structure and Navigation

- **Chapter Overview:**
  At the beginning of each chapter, you will find a brief summary outlining the key topics and learning outcomes. This helps you know what to expect and allows you to focus on the concepts that are most relevant to your needs.
- **Interactive Diagrams & Visual Aids:**
  Throughout the book, you'll encounter diagrams and flowcharts that visually represent complex concepts. These visuals are designed to reinforce the written material and provide a clearer understanding of how different elements of agentic AI interact.
- **Real-World Examples & Case Studies:**
  Practical examples and case studies are integrated into the chapters. They not only illustrate how theoretical concepts are applied in real-world scenarios but also help you relate the material to your own experiences.
- **Hands-On Exercises:**
  Each section concludes with exercises and projects that encourage you to apply what you've learned. These exercises include code examples, quick quizzes, and reflective questions designed to test your understanding.

Learning Outcomes

For each chapter, you will find a "Learning Outcomes" section that clearly states what you should be able to do or understand after reading the chapter. This includes:

- **Key Concepts:** What fundamental ideas you should know.
- **Technical Skills:** Specific tools, techniques, or methodologies introduced.
- **Practical Applications:** How to apply these concepts in real-world situations.
- **Critical Thinking:** Questions or exercises to encourage deeper reflection on the material.

Below is an example table for learning outcomes that you might see at the start of a chapter:

Learning Outcome	Description
Understand the core principles of agentic AI	Grasp the key definitions and concepts behind autonomous systems.
Identify real-world applications	Recognize how agentic AI is used across various industries.
Build a simple autonomous agent	Follow a step-by-step guide to implement a basic AI system.
Analyze ethical implications	Evaluate the ethical, legal, and social issues surrounding AI adoption.

Using Interactive Diagrams

Interactive diagrams in this book are meant to serve as dynamic visual representations of the content. For example, the following Python code snippet demonstrates how you might generate a flowchart of the book's structure using the NetworkX and Matplotlib libraries:

python

```
import networkx as nx
```

```python
import matplotlib.pyplot as plt

# Create a directed graph representing the structure of the book
G = nx.DiGraph()

# Define nodes corresponding to the key chapters/sections
nodes = [
    "Introduction", "Foundations", "Mechanics", "Data",
    "Developing Agentic AI", "Applications", "Workplace",
    "Ethics", "Decision Making", "Troubleshooting",
    "Interactive Tools", "Future of AI", "Conclusion"
]
G.add_nodes_from(nodes)

# Define edges to illustrate the flow between sections
edges = [
    ("Introduction", "Foundations"),
    ("Foundations", "Mechanics"),
    ("Mechanics", "Data"),
    ("Data", "Developing Agentic AI"),
    ("Developing Agentic AI", "Applications"),
    ("Applications", "Workplace"),
    ("Workplace", "Ethics"),
```

```
    ("Ethics", "Decision Making"),

    ("Decision Making", "Troubleshooting"),

    ("Troubleshooting", "Interactive Tools"),

    ("Interactive Tools", "Future of AI"),

    ("Future of AI", "Conclusion")

]

G.add_edges_from(edges)


# Draw the graph with labels and directional arrows

plt.figure(figsize=(10, 6))

pos = nx.spring_layout(G, seed=42)  # Seed for reproducibility of layout

nx.draw(G, pos, with_labels=True, node_size=2000,
node_color="skyblue", font_size=10, arrows=True)

plt.title("Interactive Diagram: Book Structure & Learning Outcomes")

plt.show()
```

Explanation of the Code:

- **Graph Creation:**
  We use a directed graph to represent the flow from one section of the book to the next.
- **Nodes and Edges:**
  Each node represents a major section or chapter, and the edges illustrate the logical progression through the book.
- **Visualization:**
  The graph is drawn using Matplotlib. The layout is arranged for clarity using spring_layout, which positions nodes in a way that minimizes overlapping edges.
- **Interactivity:**
  While this code creates a static diagram, similar interactive versions (e.g., using

Plotly or web-based tools) can be integrated into an online companion website for the book. QR codes in the print edition can link to these interactive visuals.

How to Engage With the Guide

1. **Read Actively:**
   As you read, pause to review diagrams and tables. Take notes on key learning outcomes and reflect on the real-world examples provided.
2. **Participate in Exercises:**
   Work through the hands-on exercises and code examples. This active participation reinforces learning and gives you practical skills.
3. **Review and Reflect:**
   At the end of each chapter, revisit the learning outcomes and check your understanding through quizzes or discussion questions.
4. **Explore Further:**
   Use the additional resources and online interactive diagrams to deepen your understanding and see updated examples of agentic AI in action.

By following these guidelines, you will not only read the content but also actively engage with the material, making your learning experience both comprehensive and enjoyable.

Chapter 2 A Brief History of Artificial Intelligence

2.1. Early Concepts and Milestones

Foundational Ideas and Pioneering Work

The seeds of artificial intelligence were planted long before modern computers existed. Early philosophers and mathematicians speculated about machines that could mimic human thought and reasoning. Two key foundational ideas include:

- **Mechanical Reasoning:**
  Philosophers like René Descartes and Gottfried Wilhelm Leibniz discussed the concept of machines that could reason logically. These ideas laid the groundwork for later mathematical and computational theories.
- **Turing's Vision:**
  In the 1940s, British mathematician Alan Turing introduced the concept of a "universal machine" capable of performing any computation given the right instructions. His 1950 paper, *"Computing Machinery and Intelligence,"* proposed what is now known as the Turing Test—a criterion for determining whether a machine exhibits human-like intelligence.

Key Milestones in Early AI

Several landmark events in the mid-20th century established the direction and potential of AI:

Year	Milestone	Significance
1950	**Turing Test Introduced**	Proposed a practical way to measure a machine's ability to exhibit intelligent behavior.
1956	**Dartmouth Conference**	Considered the birth of AI as an academic discipline; brought together

		researchers who coined the term "artificial intelligence."
1960s	**Early AI Programs (e.g., ELIZA, DENDRAL)**	ELIZA simulated conversation; DENDRAL provided early examples of expert systems in specific domains (chemistry).
1970s	**Development of Expert Systems**	Expert systems like MYCIN in medicine emerged, showing that computers could mimic expert-level decision-making.

Explanation of Milestones:

- **The Dartmouth Conference (1956):**
  Often cited as the founding event of artificial intelligence, this summer workshop gathered computer scientists, mathematicians, and cognitive scientists. Participants were optimistic about the potential of machines to replicate aspects of human intelligence. The conference set the agenda for AI research, leading to the development of programs that could solve algebra problems, prove theorems, and even play games.
- **Early AI Programs:**
  - **ELIZA (1966):**
    Developed by Joseph Weizenbaum, ELIZA was one of the first programs to mimic human conversation using pattern matching and scripted responses. Although simple by today's standards, it demonstrated the potential of natural language processing.
  - **DENDRAL (1965):**
    A program designed for chemical analysis, DENDRAL used heuristics to help chemists determine the structure of molecules. It marked one of the earliest instances of AI being applied in a specialized field.

These early concepts and programs not only captured the imagination of researchers and the public but also laid the groundwork for the more complex AI systems that would follow.

2.2. From Reactive Systems to Autonomous Agents

Reactive Systems: The Early Approach

In the initial stages of AI research, many systems were designed to be "reactive." Reactive systems operate on the principle of responding directly to inputs from their environment without the need for internal state or long-term planning. Characteristics include:

- **Immediate Response:**
  The system analyzes current inputs and produces a corresponding output. There is little or no memory of past events.
- **Simplicity:**
  These systems rely on pre-defined rules and simple decision trees. For example, a basic robotic vacuum might change direction when encountering an obstacle.
- **Limitations:**
  While effective in controlled environments, reactive systems struggle with complex tasks that require planning or learning from past experiences.

Transition to Autonomous Agents

Over time, the limitations of reactive systems led researchers to develop more sophisticated architectures—systems that could not only respond to their environment but also plan, learn, and adapt. This evolution gave rise to autonomous agents. Key developments include:

- **Introduction of Memory and Learning:**
  Autonomous agents incorporate elements of memory, allowing them to store information about past interactions. They use learning algorithms—such as reinforcement learning—to improve decision-making over time.
- **Goal-Oriented Behavior:**
  Unlike reactive systems, autonomous agents are designed to pursue specific goals. They are capable of evaluating different courses of action and selecting the one most likely to achieve a desired outcome.
- **Dynamic Decision-Making:**
  These systems are not limited to pre-programmed responses. They continuously

assess the environment, update their internal models, and adapt to new conditions.

Comparing Reactive Systems and Autonomous Agents

Below is a comparison table that outlines the differences between reactive systems and autonomous agents:

Aspect	Reactive Systems	Autonomous Agents
Memory	Little to no memory; operates on immediate input	Retains information from previous interactions for learning
Decision-Making	Rule-based and fixed responses	Dynamic and goal-oriented decision-making
Learning Capability	Typically absent	Uses algorithms (e.g., reinforcement learning) to adapt
Complexity of Tasks	Suited for simple, predictable tasks	Capable of handling complex and changing environments
Flexibility	Low	High; can plan and adjust strategies based on outcomes

Real-World Example of the Transition

Consider the evolution in robotics:

- **Reactive Robotics:**
  Early robots, such as basic automated assembly line arms, were programmed to perform repetitive tasks without deviation. They reacted to physical inputs—like a sensor detecting an object—and executed a pre-set motion.
- **Autonomous Robotics:**
  Modern autonomous robots, such as self-driving cars, incorporate sophisticated sensor arrays, real-time data processing, and learning algorithms. They continuously analyze their surroundings, predict the actions of other vehicles, and make decisions based on a combination of programmed rules and learned behaviors.

Simple Code Example: Reactive vs. Autonomous Decision-Making

Below is a simplified Python example that contrasts a reactive system with an autonomous agent in a simulated environment:

python

```python
import random


# Reactive System: Acts solely based on current input

def reactive_system(sensor_input):

    if sensor_input > 0:

        return "Move Right"

    elif sensor_input < 0:

        return "Move Left"

    else:

        return "Stay"


# Autonomous Agent: Uses past experience to make decisions

class AutonomousAgent:
```

```python
    def __init__(self):

        self.memory = []


    def perceive(self, sensor_input):

        # Save the sensor input to memory for future learning

        self.memory.append(sensor_input)

        return sensor_input


    def decide(self, sensor_input):

        # Use a simple rule with memory: if input is consistently positive, move right; if negative, move left

        if sum(self.memory[-3:]) > 0:

            return "Move Right"

        elif sum(self.memory[-3:]) < 0:

            return "Move Left"

        else:

            return "Stay"


# Simulation: Compare both systems with random inputs

inputs = [random.choice([-1, 0, 1]) for _ in range(10)]

print("Sensor Inputs:", inputs)

print("Reactive System Decisions:")

for inp in inputs:

    print(reactive_system(inp))
```

```
print("\nAutonomous Agent Decisions:")

agent = AutonomousAgent()

for inp in inputs:

    sensor = agent.perceive(inp)

    decision = agent.decide(sensor)

    print(decision)
```

Explanation of the Code:

- **Reactive System:**
  The function reactive_system simply checks the current sensor input and returns
  an action based on that input, without considering previous data.
- **Autonomous Agent:**
  The AutonomousAgent class keeps a memory of recent sensor inputs. In the
  decide method, it uses the sum of the last three inputs as a simple heuristic to
  determine a more informed action. This demonstrates how even basic memory
  and aggregation can help an agent make better decisions over time.

2.3. The Evolution of Machine Learning and Deep Learning

From Early Statistical Models to Modern Neural Networks

The field of artificial intelligence has undergone a significant transformation, especially
over the past few decades. Initially, AI research focused on symbolic reasoning and rule-
based systems. However, as data became more abundant and computing power
increased, a new approach known as machine learning (ML) emerged. Machine learning
allowed systems to learn from data rather than being explicitly programmed with a set
of rules.

Early Machine Learning

- **Statistical Foundations:**
  Early ML methods were grounded in statistics. Algorithms such as linear
  regression, logistic regression, and decision trees were developed to find patterns

in data and make predictions. These techniques were relatively simple, interpretable, and effective for many applications.

- **Feature Engineering:**
A critical step in classical ML was the manual selection and transformation of features. Experts would decide which aspects of the data were most important, often using domain knowledge. Although this approach worked well, it was time-consuming and limited by the quality of human insight.

The Advent of Deep Learning

- **Neural Networks Resurgence:**
Although neural networks have been studied since the 1950s, their true potential was limited by hardware constraints and the lack of large datasets. With the advent of big data and GPUs, deep learning—neural networks with many layers—resurfaced as a transformative technology.
- **Key Innovations:**
  - **Convolutional Neural Networks (CNNs):** Revolutionized image processing by automatically learning spatial hierarchies of features.
  - **Recurrent Neural Networks (RNNs) and LSTM Networks:** Enabled breakthroughs in sequential data processing, such as language translation and time-series analysis.
  - **Transformer Models:** Introduced in the past few years, these models have redefined natural language processing (NLP) by allowing parallel processing of data and capturing long-range dependencies in text.

Comparison: Classical Machine Learning vs. Deep Learning

The following table summarizes key differences between classical machine learning approaches and modern deep learning techniques:

Aspect	Classical Machine Learning	Deep Learning
Feature Engineering	Manual, domain-specific feature selection required	Automatically learns feature representations from raw data

Model Complexity	Typically shallow models (e.g., decision trees, SVM)	Multi-layered architectures (deep neural networks)
Data Requirements	Effective with moderate-sized datasets	Requires large amounts of data for optimal performance
Computational Needs	Generally lower; can run on standard CPUs	Often computationally intensive; benefits from GPUs/TPUs
Interpretability	More interpretable and easier to explain	Often considered "black boxes" with complex internal representations

A Simple Code Example: Building a Basic Neural Network

Below is an example using Python and the Keras library to demonstrate a simple neural network. This code trains a model on the Iris dataset—a classic dataset used for classification tasks.

python

```python
# Import necessary libraries

import numpy as np

from sklearn.datasets import load_iris

from sklearn.model_selection import train_test_split

from sklearn.preprocessing import OneHotEncoder, StandardScaler

from tensorflow.keras.models import Sequential

from tensorflow.keras.layers import Dense
```

```python
from tensorflow.keras.optimizers import Adam


# Load the Iris dataset
iris = load_iris()
X = iris.data  # Features
y = iris.target.reshape(-1, 1)  # Labels


# One-hot encode the target variable
encoder = OneHotEncoder(sparse=False)
y_encoded = encoder.fit_transform(y)


# Standardize the features
scaler = StandardScaler()
X_scaled = scaler.fit_transform(X)


# Split the data into training and testing sets
X_train, X_test, y_train, y_test = train_test_split(X_scaled, y_encoded,
test_size=0.2, random_state=42)


# Define a simple neural network model
model = Sequential([
    Dense(10, activation='relu', input_shape=(X_train.shape[1],)),  # Hidden layer with 10 neurons

    Dense(10, activation='relu'),                    # Second hidden layer
```

```python
    Dense(3, activation='softmax')                    # Output layer for 3
classes

])


# Compile the model

model.compile(optimizer=Adam(learning_rate=0.01),
loss='categorical_crossentropy', metrics=['accuracy'])


# Train the model

history = model.fit(X_train, y_train, epochs=50, batch_size=5,
validation_split=0.2, verbose=1)


# Evaluate the model on the test data

test_loss, test_accuracy = model.evaluate(X_test, y_test, verbose=0)

print(f"Test Accuracy: {test_accuracy:.2f}")


# Explanation:

# - The model is defined with two hidden layers using ReLU activation and
an output layer using softmax.

# - The Adam optimizer is used with a learning rate of 0.01.

# - The model is trained for 50 epochs, and accuracy is evaluated on a test
split.
```

Explanation of the Code:

- **Data Preparation:**
  The Iris dataset is loaded and preprocessed. Labels are one-hot encoded for multi-class classification, and features are standardized for better performance.
- **Model Definition:**
  A Sequential model is defined with two hidden layers. The hidden layers use the ReLU activation function to introduce non-linearity, while the output layer uses softmax for class probability distribution.
- **Training and Evaluation:**
  The model is compiled with the Adam optimizer and trained using categorical crossentropy loss. Finally, the model is evaluated on the test set, with the test accuracy printed as a measure of performance.

2.4. Lessons from the Past: What History Teaches Us About AI

Insights Gained Over Decades of AI Research

The evolution of AI offers many valuable lessons that can guide current and future research and development. By reflecting on past successes and failures, researchers and practitioners can better navigate the challenges of today's rapidly advancing technologies.

Key Lessons Learned

1. **The Importance of Data:**
   - **Lesson:** Early AI systems were limited by the quality and quantity of available data. As data became more accessible and voluminous, machine learning advanced significantly.
   - **Implication:** For modern AI systems, ensuring high-quality, diverse, and well-labeled data is essential. Data is the foundation upon which effective learning models are built.
2. **Balancing Complexity and Interpretability:**
   - **Lesson:** Early, simpler models were more interpretable and easier to troubleshoot. As models grew more complex (like deep neural networks), their "black-box" nature often made them harder to understand.
   - **Implication:** There is a growing need for techniques that improve the transparency of complex models, such as explainable AI, to build trust and facilitate debugging.
3. **The Role of Computation:**

- **Lesson:** Advances in computational power, such as GPUs and specialized hardware, have driven significant breakthroughs in AI, particularly in deep learning.
- **Implication:** Future innovations in hardware and parallel computing will continue to expand the capabilities of AI systems, enabling more sophisticated models and faster training times.

4. **Interdisciplinary Collaboration:**
   - **Lesson:** Early AI research benefited from the collaboration of computer scientists, mathematicians, cognitive scientists, and domain experts. The breakthroughs were often the result of cross-disciplinary efforts.
   - **Implication:** Modern AI development should continue to foster collaboration among diverse fields, combining technical expertise with insights from ethics, psychology, and domain-specific knowledge.

5. **Learning from Failure:**
   - **Lesson:** The AI winters—periods when progress slowed and funding dried up—remind us that overhyping technology without delivering practical results can lead to disillusionment.
   - **Implication:** Setting realistic expectations, continuously validating results, and iterating on feedback are crucial for sustainable progress in AI.

A Summary Table of Lessons from History

Lesson	Historical Example	Modern Implication
Data is Key	Early ML models struggled with limited datasets	Invest in quality data and robust data pipelines
Interpretability vs. Complexity	Rule-based systems were simple but limited; deep nets are complex but opaque	Develop explainable AI methods to enhance model transparency
Advances in Computation	Transition from CPU-bound systems to GPU-accelerated models	Leverage modern hardware for efficient training and model scaling

Interdisciplinary Collaboration	The Dartmouth Conference and subsequent collaborative research	Foster multi-disciplinary teams to drive innovative AI solutions
Managing Expectations	AI winters due to unmet promises and overhype	Set realistic goals, validate claims, and build trust incrementally

Reflecting on the Journey

The history of machine learning and deep learning is a testament to the power of iterative improvement and learning from past challenges. Early experiments, though primitive by today's standards, provided a critical foundation for later breakthroughs. Modern AI systems benefit from decades of accumulated knowledge, and many of the challenges faced in the past still echo today—albeit at a much larger scale.

By understanding these lessons, researchers and practitioners can better appreciate the evolution of the field and anticipate future trends. This historical perspective not only honors the pioneering work that has brought us to this point but also informs the ethical and practical considerations that will shape the next generation of AI technologies.

3. Foundations of Agentic AI

Understanding agentic AI starts with a solid grasp of the fundamental definitions, terms, and building blocks that form autonomous systems. This section breaks down essential concepts and explains the core components that allow these systems to perceive, decide, and act independently.

Chapter 3 Foundations of Agentic AI

3.1. Key Definitions and Terminology (Beginner's Tip Sections)

Before diving into the technical aspects of agentic AI, it's important to familiarize yourself with the key terms and concepts. Below is a list of fundamental definitions along with beginner's tips for each term.

Term	Definition	Beginner's Tip
Agentic AI	AI systems that operate with a degree of autonomy by making decisions and taking actions without constant human input.	Think of agentic AI as a "smart assistant" that plans and acts on its own.
Autonomy	The capacity of a system to operate independently, making decisions based on internal goals and environmental inputs.	Autonomy is similar to how a self-driving car navigates without manual control.
Reactive System	A system that responds directly to inputs with pre-programmed actions, without memory of past events or the ability to plan ahead.	Reactive systems are like simple thermostats that adjust temperature based only on current readings.
Learning (Machine Learning)	The process by which systems improve their performance over time by analyzing data and identifying patterns, rather	Imagine learning to ride a bike—you get better with practice and experience.

than following strictly pre-defined rules.

Adaptability	The ability of an AI system to adjust its behavior based on new information or changing conditions, often achieved through continuous learning.	Adaptability in AI is like a smartphone app that updates itself based on user behavior.
Decision-Making	The mechanism through which an AI system evaluates data and selects an action among multiple possibilities, often using algorithms or learned models.	Consider decision-making as similar to choosing the fastest route on a map app.
Perception	The process by which an AI system collects and interprets data from its environment, typically through sensors or data inputs.	Perception in AI is akin to human senses (like sight and hearing) gathering information about the world.
Actuation	The execution of actions in the physical or digital world, as determined by the system's decision-making processes.	Think of actuation as the "motor" of an AI that carries out decisions (e.g., moving a robotic arm).

Beginner's Tip:
When reading about these concepts, try to relate them to everyday technologies—such as smartphones, smart home devices, or even simple appliances—to better understand how these ideas manifest in real-world systems.

3.2. Core Components of Autonomous Systems

Autonomous systems, such as those powered by agentic AI, rely on several key components that work together to enable independent operation. Below is an overview of these components along with a simple code example to illustrate how they might interact in a basic simulation.

1. Perception

Definition:
Perception involves gathering data from the environment through sensors (or data sources) and interpreting that data to understand the current state.

- **Sensors:** Cameras, microphones, LIDAR, temperature sensors, or digital data feeds.
- **Data Processing:** Algorithms that process raw sensor data into meaningful information (e.g., edge detection in images).

2. Decision-Making

Definition:
This component processes the information gathered during perception to make informed choices. Decision-making often uses algorithms such as rule-based systems, machine learning models, or reinforcement learning strategies.

- **Algorithms:** Decision trees, reinforcement learning, or neural networks.
- **Planning:** Evaluating potential actions based on goals and predicted outcomes.

3. Actuation

Definition:
Actuation is the execution of decisions through physical or digital actions. It involves controlling devices, sending commands, or initiating processes based on the decisions made.

- **Motors and Controllers:** In robotics, these translate decisions into movement.
- **Digital Commands:** In software systems, actions might include data manipulation, sending notifications, or interfacing with other services.

4. Learning and Adaptation

Definition:

Learning mechanisms allow the system to improve over time. By analyzing outcomes of past actions, an autonomous system can adjust its decision-making strategy to enhance performance.

- **Feedback Loops:** Continuous monitoring of outcomes to refine behavior.
- **Machine Learning Models:** Algorithms that update parameters based on experience.

5. Memory and Data Storage

Definition:

Memory allows autonomous systems to store past information and experiences. This historical data is crucial for improving decision-making and adapting to new situations.

- **Short-term Memory:** Immediate storage of recent data for quick reference.
- **Long-term Memory:** Databases or models that capture trends over time for strategic learning.

A Simple Simulation Example

Below is a Python example that simulates an autonomous agent combining perception, decision-making, and actuation. This example builds on a simple scenario where the agent receives sensor inputs, makes a decision, and acts accordingly.

python

```python
import random


class AutonomousAgent:

    def __init__(self, goal):

        self.goal = goal     # Target value the agent tries to reach

        self.position = 0     # Initial position

        self.memory = []     # Memory to store recent sensor inputs
```

```python
def perceive(self):
    # Simulate a sensor reading: the difference between current position
    # and goal with some noise
    sensor_input = (self.goal - self.position) + random.uniform(-0.5, 0.5)
    self.memory.append(sensor_input)
    print(f"Perceived sensor input: {sensor_input:.2f}")
    return sensor_input


def decide(self, sensor_input):
    # Decision-making: if sensor input is positive, move right; if negative,
    # move left
    if sensor_input > 0:
        decision = "Move Right"
    elif sensor_input < 0:
        decision = "Move Left"
    else:
        decision = "Stay"
    print(f"Decision: {decision}")
    return decision


def act(self, decision):
    # Actuation: update the position based on the decision
    if decision == "Move Right":
```

```python
            self.position += 1
        elif decision == "Move Left":
            self.position -= 1
        print(f"Actuated action. New position: {self.position}")


    def run(self, steps=10):
        # Run the autonomous loop for a fixed number of steps
        print(f"Starting simulation. Goal: {self.goal}, Initial Position: {self.position}\n")
        for step in range(steps):
            print(f"--- Step {step + 1} ---")
            sensor_input = self.perceive()
            decision = self.decide(sensor_input)
            self.act(decision)
            print("")
        print("Simulation completed.")


# Example usage:
if __name__ == "__main__":
    agent = AutonomousAgent(goal=5)
    agent.run(steps=10)
```

Explanation of the Code:

- **Perception:**
  The perceive method simulates a sensor reading by calculating the difference between the current position and the goal, with added randomness to mimic noise in real sensor data. The sensor input is stored in the agent's memory.
- **Decision-Making:**
  The decide method uses a simple rule: if the sensor input is positive (indicating the goal is to the right), it decides to move right; if negative, it moves left; if zero, it stays in place. This is a basic example of goal-oriented decision-making.
- **Actuation:**
  The act method translates the decision into a change in position. Moving right increases the position, while moving left decreases it.
- **Simulation Loop:**
  The run method simulates the autonomous system over a number of steps, allowing you to see how the agent perceives its environment, makes decisions, and acts over time.

Summary:
This section has provided a thorough introduction to the foundational concepts of agentic AI. We defined key terms with beginner-friendly tips and explained the core components—perception, decision-making, actuation, learning, and memory—that enable autonomous systems. The provided table and code example illustrate how these elements work together in practice, offering a solid base for further exploration into agentic AI.

3.3. Comparing Agentic, Reactive, and Cognitive AI

Artificial intelligence systems can be broadly classified based on their capabilities and methods of operation. In this section, we compare three important paradigms: Agentic AI, Reactive AI, and Cognitive AI. Understanding these differences is key to grasping how modern autonomous systems fit within the larger AI landscape.

Overview of the Three Paradigms

- **Reactive AI:**
  Reactive systems are the simplest form of AI. They respond directly to inputs from the environment using pre-defined rules, with no memory or learning from past experiences. These systems operate in a "stimulus-response" manner. *Example:* A basic thermostat that adjusts temperature based solely on the current reading.

- **Agentic AI:**
  Agentic AI represents systems that possess a degree of autonomy. They are not only reactive but also include components like memory, learning, and decision-making that enable them to adapt and pursue goals over time.
  Example: A self-driving car that continuously adjusts its behavior based on sensor inputs, past driving experiences, and a target destination.
- **Cognitive AI:**
  Cognitive AI systems aim to mimic human thought processes by incorporating elements of reasoning, understanding, and sometimes even emotions. These systems are designed to handle complex, ambiguous tasks by simulating aspects of human cognition, such as planning and natural language understanding.
  Example: An AI personal assistant that can engage in natural dialogue, learn from interactions, and provide nuanced responses similar to human conversation.

Comparative Table

The following table outlines key differences between these paradigms:

Aspect	Reactive AI	Agentic AI	Cognitive AI
Memory	No memory; acts on immediate input only	Maintains short-term or long-term memory for learning	Mimics human memory and reasoning processes
Learning Ability	Lacks learning; relies on pre-set rules	Incorporates learning (e.g., reinforcement learning)	Uses advanced learning techniques, including contextual and semantic learning
Decision-Making	Simple, rule-based decisions	Goal-oriented decisions with adaptive strategies	Complex decision-making that

			simulates human thought
Complexity	Low; suitable for predictable, repetitive tasks	Moderate; handles dynamic and changing environments	High; designed for complex, ambiguous, and nuanced tasks
Example Systems	Basic sensors, thermostats, simple robots	Autonomous vehicles, robotic assistants	Advanced virtual assistants, systems for natural language understanding, cognitive robotics

Illustrative Code Example

Below is a simplified Python example that demonstrates the three paradigms using a common interface. Each class represents a different style of decision-making:

python

```python
class ReactiveAI:
    def decide(self, input_signal):
        # Reactive AI: Responds solely to the current input
        if input_signal > 0:
            return "Move Right"
        elif input_signal < 0:
            return "Move Left"
        else:
```

```python
        return "Stay"


class AgenticAI:
    def __init__(self):
        self.memory = []


    def decide(self, input_signal):
        # Store input in memory for simple learning
        self.memory.append(input_signal)
        # Agentic AI: Consider recent inputs to decide action
        avg_signal = sum(self.memory[-3:]) / len(self.memory[-3:])
        if avg_signal > 0:
            return "Move Right"
        elif avg_signal < 0:
            return "Move Left"
        else:
            return "Stay"


class CognitiveAI:
    def decide(self, input_signal):
        # Cognitive AI: Simulates a more nuanced decision-making process
        # For demonstration, using a conditional structure that could represent a more complex evaluation
        if input_signal > 0.5:
```

```python
        return "Execute advanced maneuver: Accelerate and steer right"
    elif input_signal < -0.5:
        return "Execute advanced maneuver: Decelerate and steer left"
    else:
        return "Hold position and analyze further"


# Simulation: Comparing the decisions made by each AI type
input_signals = [0.7, -0.3, 0.1, -0.8, 0.4]
print("Comparing AI Decisions:")
for signal in input_signals:
    reactive_decision = ReactiveAI().decide(signal)
    agentic_decision = AgenticAI().decide(signal)
    cognitive_decision = CognitiveAI().decide(signal)
    print(f"Input Signal: {signal:.2f}")
    print(f"  Reactive AI Decision: {reactive_decision}")
    print(f"  Agentic AI Decision: {agentic_decision}")
    print(f"  Cognitive AI Decision: {cognitive_decision}\n")
```

Explanation of the Code:

- **ReactiveAI Class:**
  Uses only the current input to decide whether to move right, left, or stay. It represents the simplest form of decision-making.
- **AgenticAI Class:**
  Maintains a short-term memory (list of recent inputs) and calculates an average to inform its decision. This simple learning mechanism mimics adaptive, goal-oriented behavior.

- **CognitiveAI Class:**
  Implements a more complex decision-making process that could be expanded with further logic or models to simulate human-like reasoning. Here, decisions are more nuanced, reflecting higher cognitive processing.
- **Simulation:**
  The simulation iterates over a series of input signals and prints the decisions of each AI type, clearly demonstrating the differences between reactive, agentic, and cognitive approaches.

3.4. Learning Outcomes: What You'll Master in This Chapter

By the end of this chapter, you will have a strong foundation in the essential concepts of agentic AI. Here are the key learning outcomes you can expect:

- **Understand Key Definitions:**
  - Comprehend the meanings of terms such as agentic AI, autonomy, learning, decision-making, perception, and actuation.
  - Recognize the importance of each term and how they contribute to the overall functioning of autonomous systems.
- **Differentiate AI Paradigms:**
  - Clearly distinguish between reactive, agentic, and cognitive AI.
  - Understand the strengths and limitations of each paradigm through comparative analysis.
- **Analyze Core Components:**
  - Gain insight into the building blocks of autonomous systems, including perception, decision-making, actuation, learning, and memory.
  - Understand how these components interact to form a cohesive, autonomous system.
- **Practical Application:**
  - Learn how to apply these concepts in simple code examples, demonstrating the differences in decision-making strategies.
  - Develop the ability to assess which type of AI system might be most appropriate for a given application.
- **Critical Thinking:**
  - Reflect on the evolution of AI paradigms and consider how historical approaches inform current technologies.
  - Prepare to integrate this foundational knowledge into more advanced topics later in the book.

Summary Table of Learning Outcomes

Learning Outcome	Description
Comprehend Key Definitions	Understand essential AI terms and their roles in autonomous systems.
Differentiate AI Paradigms	Clearly identify the differences between reactive, agentic, and cognitive AI.
Analyze Core Components	Recognize how perception, decision-making, actuation, learning, and memory form the backbone of AI systems.
Apply Concepts Practically	Work with code examples to see how these paradigms operate in practice.
Develop Critical Thinking	Evaluate the historical and modern context of AI to inform future learning and application.

This section provides an exhaustive explanation of the three AI paradigms, supported by a comparison table and a code example. It also outlines clear learning outcomes that detail what you will master by the end of the chapter. The information is presented in a clear, accessible style suitable for both beginners and tech professionals.

Chapter 4 The Mechanics Behind Agentic AI

Agentic AI systems are built on a combination of sophisticated algorithms and learning models that allow them to perceive their environment, make decisions, and act autonomously. This section explains the underlying mechanics that drive such systems.

4.1. Algorithms Driving Autonomy

Overview

At the core of autonomous systems are algorithms designed to process inputs, evaluate options, and make decisions that align with a specific goal. These algorithms can be broadly classified into two categories:

1. **Rule-Based Algorithms:**
   - **Definition:** These algorithms follow pre-defined rules and logic to generate responses.
   - **Characteristics:**
     - Simple and predictable
     - No capacity to learn or adapt beyond their initial programming
   - **Example:** A thermostat that turns on the heating when the temperature drops below a set threshold.
2. **Learning-Based Algorithms:**
   - **Definition:** These algorithms use data to learn and improve over time.
   - **Characteristics:**
     - Adaptability to new scenarios
     - Use of techniques such as supervised learning, unsupervised learning, and reinforcement learning
   - **Example:** An autonomous vehicle that adjusts its driving strategy based on past experiences and changing road conditions.

Key Components of Autonomous Algorithms

Component	Description	Example

Input Processing	Gathers and processes data from sensors or digital sources.	Processing camera images or sensor readings.
Decision-Making	Evaluates the processed data to choose a course of action using logic, models, or learning techniques.	Choosing to brake or steer in a self-driving car.
Feedback Loop	Incorporates outcomes of actions to refine future decisions.	Adjusting driving strategy based on successful navigation.
Adaptability	Ability to modify behavior based on past performance and new data.	Learning to avoid obstacles more effectively over time.

Example: Simple Decision Algorithm

Below is a simple Python example that shows a decision-making algorithm using if-else statements, which is a basic form of rule-based autonomy:

python

```python
def basic_decision(sensor_input):

    """

    A simple decision algorithm that determines action based on sensor
input.


    Parameters:

    sensor_input (float): The value indicating the difference from the target.
```

```python
    Returns:
        str: Action to be taken.
    """
    if sensor_input > 0:
        return "Move Right"
    elif sensor_input < 0:
        return "Move Left"
    else:
        return "Stay"


# Example usage:
input_value = 1.5  # Simulated sensor reading indicating target is to the right

action = basic_decision(input_value)

print(f"Sensor input: {input_value}, Action: {action}")
```

Explanation:

- **Input Processing:** The function basic_decision accepts a numerical sensor input.
- **Decision-Making:** It then uses a series of if-else statements to decide whether to "Move Right," "Move Left," or "Stay."
- **Output:** This is a basic demonstration of a rule-based algorithm that forms the foundation of more complex decision systems.

4.2. Neural Networks and Reinforcement Learning

Overview

While rule-based algorithms offer a straightforward approach, modern agentic AI systems often leverage learning-based techniques to handle complex and dynamic environments. Two of the most influential techniques are:

1. **Neural Networks:**
   - **Definition:** Computational models inspired by the human brain, consisting of interconnected nodes (neurons) organized in layers.
   - **Purpose:** Automatically learn feature representations from raw data, enabling the system to recognize patterns and make predictions.
   - **Application:** Image recognition, natural language processing, and even decision-making in autonomous systems.
2. **Reinforcement Learning (RL):**
   - **Definition:** A learning paradigm where an agent learns to make decisions by taking actions in an environment to maximize a reward signal.
   - **Purpose:** Enables an agent to learn optimal behaviors through trial and error, receiving feedback in the form of rewards or penalties.
   - **Application:** Autonomous driving, game playing (e.g., AlphaGo), and robotic control.

Neural Networks: Basic Structure

Neural networks are typically composed of three main layers:

Layer Type	Description	Function
Input Layer	Receives raw data inputs (e.g., images, sensor readings).	Passes data to the network for processing.
Hidden Layers	Consist of neurons that transform inputs via weighted connections and activation functions.	Extract features and patterns from the data.

| Output Layer | Produces the final result, such as classification or a decision. | Provides actionable outputs (e.g., class label, action). |

Reinforcement Learning: Key Concepts

Concept	Description
Agent	The learner or decision-maker.
Environment	The context within which the agent operates.
State	A representation of the current situation of the agent within the environment.
Action	What the agent can do at any given state.
Reward	Feedback received after taking an action.
Policy	A strategy that defines the agent's behavior at a given state.

Example: Simple Reinforcement Learning with Q-Learning

Below is a simplified Python example of a Q-learning algorithm applied to a basic grid-world environment:

python

```python
import numpy as np
import random

# Define the grid-world dimensions and possible actions
grid_size = 5
actions = ["up", "down", "left", "right"]

# Initialize the Q-table with zeros (rows: states, columns: actions)
q_table = np.zeros((grid_size * grid_size, len(actions)))

def state_to_index(row, col):
    """Converts grid coordinates to state index."""
    return row * grid_size + col

def choose_action(state, epsilon=0.1):
    """Choose an action using epsilon-greedy strategy."""
    if random.uniform(0, 1) < epsilon:
        return random.choice(range(len(actions)))  # Explore
    else:
        return np.argmax(q_table[state])           # Exploit
```

```python
# Hyperparameters
alpha = 0.1      # Learning rate
gamma = 0.9      # Discount factor
epsilon = 0.1    # Exploration rate
episodes = 100


# Simulation: Simple grid-world environment
for episode in range(episodes):
    # Start at a random position
    row, col = random.randint(0, grid_size - 1), random.randint(0, grid_size - 1)
    state = state_to_index(row, col)


    for _ in range(50):  # Limit number of steps per episode
        action_index = choose_action(state, epsilon)
        action = actions[action_index]


        # Simulate moving in the grid: update row, col based on action
        new_row, new_col = row, col
        if action == "up" and row > 0:
            new_row -= 1
        elif action == "down" and row < grid_size - 1:
            new_row += 1
        elif action == "left" and col > 0:
```

```python
        new_col -= 1
    elif action == "right" and col < grid_size - 1:
        new_col += 1


    new_state = state_to_index(new_row, new_col)


    # Reward: +1 for reaching the bottom-right corner; otherwise 0
    reward = 1 if (new_row == grid_size - 1 and new_col == grid_size - 1) else 0


    # Q-learning update formula
    q_table[state, action_index] = q_table[state, action_index] + alpha * (
        reward + gamma * np.max(q_table[new_state]) - q_table[state, action_index]
    )


    # Update state and position
    state = new_state
    row, col = new_row, new_col


    # End episode if goal is reached
    if reward == 1:
        break
```

```
print("Q-table after training:")

print(q_table)
```

Explanation of the Code:

- **Grid-World Environment:**
  The environment is a simple 5x5 grid where the goal is to reach the bottom-right corner. Each cell in the grid represents a state.
- **Q-Table:**
  A table (q_table) is initialized to store the Q-values for each state-action pair. The Q-values represent the expected reward for taking an action in a given state.
- **State Conversion:**
  The helper function state_to_index converts grid coordinates to a single state index for the Q-table.
- **Action Selection:**
  The choose_action function implements an epsilon-greedy strategy: with a small probability (epsilon), a random action is chosen to encourage exploration; otherwise, the best-known action is selected.
- **Q-Learning Update:**
  For each step, the agent updates the Q-value using the formula:
  $$Q(s,a)=Q(s,a)+\alpha(reward+\gamma \max_{a'}Q(s',a')-Q(s,a))Q(s,a)=Q(s,a)+\alpha(reward+\gamma a'\max Q(s',a')-Q(s,a))$$
  where $\alpha\alpha$ is the learning rate and $\gamma\gamma$ is the discount factor.
- **Simulation Loop:**
  The agent runs multiple episodes, moving through the grid and updating its Q-table until it learns the optimal policy to reach the goal.

Summary

- **Algorithms Driving Autonomy:**
  Autonomous systems rely on algorithms that process sensor inputs, make decisions, and execute actions. These algorithms can be rule-based or learning-based. A basic decision algorithm example shows how simple conditional logic can guide behavior.
- **Neural Networks and Reinforcement Learning:**
  Neural networks automatically learn patterns from data, while reinforcement learning enables an agent to learn optimal actions through interaction with an

environment. The provided Q-learning example illustrates a simple implementation of reinforcement learning in a grid-world, showcasing the mechanics behind learning-based autonomous systems.

This detailed explanation, along with tables and code examples, provides a foundational understanding of the mechanics behind agentic AI, making the concepts accessible and actionable for beginners and professionals alike.

4.3. Decision-Making Processes in Autonomous Agents

Autonomous agents rely on decision-making processes to choose appropriate actions based on sensory inputs, internal states, and predefined goals. Unlike simple rule-based systems, these processes can integrate learning, planning, and evaluation to achieve more robust and adaptive behavior.

Key Steps in the Decision-Making Process

The decision-making process in autonomous agents typically follows these steps:

1. **Perception:**
   The agent gathers data from its environment through sensors or digital inputs. This raw data is then processed to create a meaningful representation of the current state.
2. **Evaluation & Contextual Analysis:**
   Once the state is known, the agent evaluates the situation. This may involve comparing the current state against expected outcomes or goals. Advanced agents may also consider past experiences stored in memory.
3. **Planning:**
   Based on the evaluation, the agent generates possible actions. This stage may involve predicting outcomes using internal models or simulation of future states.
4. **Action Selection:**
   Among the possible actions, the agent selects the one that maximizes the expected benefit (or minimizes cost). This decision may use simple heuristics, learned policies, or a combination of both.
5. **Actuation:**
   The chosen action is then executed, whether by moving a physical component or triggering a digital process.
6. **Feedback and Learning:**
   After acting, the agent observes the outcome through feedback. This information is used to update internal models or learning algorithms, refining future decisions.

Comparative Table of Decision-Making Techniques

Stage	Description	Technique/Example
Perception	Collecting and processing environmental data	Sensor data filtering, image recognition, audio signal processing
Evaluation	Assessing the current state against goals	State estimation, risk assessment, anomaly detection
Planning	Generating possible actions based on future predictions	Path planning, decision trees, simulation models
Action Selection	Choosing the optimal action from a set of alternatives	Epsilon-greedy policy, softmax selection in reinforcement learning
Actuation	Executing the selected action	Motor commands in robotics, API calls in digital systems
Feedback & Learning	Updating the agent's knowledge base based on the outcome of the action	Q-learning updates, policy gradient adjustments

Example: Simulating a Decision-Making Loop

The following Python code simulates a simple autonomous decision-making loop. In this example, an agent attempts to move toward a target. The agent evaluates its position relative to the target, plans its next move, selects an action, and then executes that action. A feedback loop allows the agent to update its behavior based on the outcome.

python

```python
import random


class AutonomousAgent:
    def __init__(self, target_position):
        self.position = 0
        self.target = target_position
        self.memory = []  # To store past errors or sensor inputs

    def perceive(self):
        """
        Simulate perception by calculating the difference between current position and target.
        Add a small random noise to simulate sensor error.
        """
        error = (self.target - self.position) + random.uniform(-0.2, 0.2)
        self.memory.append(error)
        print(f"Perception: Error = {error:.2f}")
        return error

    def evaluate(self, error):
```

```python
    """
    Evaluate the state by analyzing the error.
    For simplicity, consider error as the key metric.
    """
    # In a real system, this step might involve more complex analysis.
    return error


def plan(self, evaluated_error):
    """
    Plan the action based on the evaluated error.
    For instance, determine the direction to move.
    """
    if evaluated_error > 0:
        planned_action = "Move Right"
    elif evaluated_error < 0:
        planned_action = "Move Left"
    else:
        planned_action = "Hold Position"
    print(f"Planning: Action = {planned_action}")
    return planned_action


def act(self, action):
    """
```

```python
    Execute the planned action by updating the position.
    """

    if action == "Move Right":
        self.position += 1
    elif action == "Move Left":
        self.position -= 1
    print(f"Actuation: New Position = {self.position}")


def feedback(self):
    """

    Provide feedback by comparing the new position to the target.

    This method can later be expanded to adjust learning parameters.
    """

    current_error = self.target - self.position

    print(f"Feedback: Current Error = {current_error}")

    return current_error


def run_decision_loop(self, steps=10):
    """

    Run the full decision-making loop for a fixed number of steps.
    """

    print(f"Starting Decision-Making Loop. Target Position = {self.target}")
    for step in range(steps):
```

```python
        print(f"\n--- Step {step + 1} ---")

        error = self.perceive()

        evaluated_error = self.evaluate(error)

        action = self.plan(evaluated_error)

        self.act(action)

        self.feedback()

    print("Decision-Making Loop Completed.")


# Example usage:
if __name__ == "__main__":

    agent = AutonomousAgent(target_position=5)

    agent.run_decision_loop(steps=10)
```

Explanation of the Code:

- **Perception:**
  The perceive method simulates sensor readings (with noise) to calculate the error between the current position and the target.
- **Evaluation & Planning:**
  The evaluate method uses the error as the primary metric, and the plan method determines the direction based on whether the error is positive or negative.
- **Actuation:**
  The act method updates the agent's position based on the planned action.
- **Feedback:**
  The feedback method outputs the current error after acting, allowing for future enhancements such as learning adjustments.
- **Loop Execution:**
  The run_decision_loop method encapsulates the entire decision-making process over multiple iterations, simulating a continuous decision loop.

4.4. Interactive Diagrams & Real-World Simulations

Interactive diagrams and simulations play a crucial role in understanding complex decision-making processes. They provide visual and practical demonstrations that complement textual explanations, making it easier to grasp how autonomous systems operate in real time.

Benefits of Interactive Diagrams

- **Visualization of Processes:**
  Diagrams help break down the decision-making flow into clear, manageable steps, illustrating the relationships between perception, planning, and action.
- **Enhanced Engagement:**
  Interactive elements encourage active learning by allowing users to experiment with different scenarios and observe the outcomes.
- **Real-World Context:**
  Simulations bridge the gap between theory and practice, showing how algorithms perform in dynamic environments. This approach makes abstract concepts more concrete and relatable.

Creating an Interactive Diagram

Below is an example using Python with the NetworkX and Matplotlib libraries to create a flowchart that visualizes the decision-making process in an autonomous agent.

python

```python
import networkx as nx

import matplotlib.pyplot as plt


def draw_decision_flowchart():

    """

    Create and display a flowchart representing the decision-making process
in an autonomous agent.

    """
```

```python
# Create a directed graph
G = nx.DiGraph()

# Define nodes representing the steps
nodes = {
    "Perception": "Collect Data",
    "Evaluation": "Analyze Error",
    "Planning": "Determine Action",
    "Action Selection": "Choose Best Action",
    "Actuation": "Execute Action",
    "Feedback": "Assess Outcome"
}

# Add nodes to the graph
for node, label in nodes.items():
    G.add_node(node, label=label)

# Define edges to represent the flow
edges = [
    ("Perception", "Evaluation"),
    ("Evaluation", "Planning"),
    ("Planning", "Action Selection"),
    ("Action Selection", "Actuation"),
```

```python
        ("Actuation", "Feedback"),

        ("Feedback", "Perception")  # Feedback loop to simulate continuous
learning
    ]

    G.add_edges_from(edges)


    # Draw the graph

    pos = nx.spring_layout(G, seed=42)

    labels = {node: f"{node}\n({data['label']})" for node, data in
G.nodes(data=True)}

    plt.figure(figsize=(10, 6))

    nx.draw(G, pos, with_labels=True, labels=labels,
node_color="lightblue", node_size=3000, arrowsize=20, font_size=10)

    plt.title("Interactive Flowchart: Decision-Making Process in Autonomous
Agents")

    plt.show()


# Example usage:

if __name__ == "__main__":

    draw_decision_flowchart()
```

Explanation of the Code:

- **Graph Construction:**
  A directed graph is created using NetworkX. Nodes represent the key stages in
  the decision-making process (e.g., Perception, Evaluation, etc.), and edges define
  the flow between these stages.

- **Labeling:**
  Each node is labeled with both the step name and a brief description (e.g., "Perception" is labeled as "Collect Data") to clarify the process.
- **Visualization:**
  The flowchart is drawn with Matplotlib. The spring layout positions the nodes for clarity, and the feedback loop is represented by an edge from Feedback back to Perception, emphasizing continuous improvement.

Real-World Simulations

In addition to static diagrams, real-world simulations allow readers to see how autonomous systems adapt to dynamic environments. For example, the decision-making loop demonstrated in section 4.3 can be extended to simulate various scenarios, such as obstacles in a robotic navigation task or fluctuating sensor inputs in a smart home system.

By combining interactive diagrams with code-based simulations, readers can:

- **Experiment:**
  Modify parameters (e.g., sensor noise, target position, learning rate) and immediately observe how these changes affect the agent's behavior.
- **Learn by Doing:**
  Gain hands-on experience with the core principles of autonomous decision-making, reinforcing theoretical concepts with practical applications.

Summary

- **Decision-Making Processes:**
  We detailed the steps—from perception and evaluation to planning, action, and feedback—that form the backbone of an autonomous agent's decision-making process. A comparative table and a Python simulation illustrate how these processes are implemented in practice.
- **Interactive Diagrams & Simulations:**
  Visual aids, like the flowchart example, help clarify the sequential and iterative nature of decision-making. Real-world simulations offer an interactive learning experience that deepens understanding and bridges theory with practical application.

This comprehensive coverage ensures that both the theory and practical aspects of decision-making in autonomous agents are accessible and well-explained, benefiting readers across varying levels of expertise.

Chapter 5. Data: The Fuel for Agentic AI

Data plays a pivotal role in the development and performance of agentic AI systems. Just as fuel powers a vehicle, high-quality data powers AI by enabling learning, decision-making, and adaptation. In this section, we explore the critical aspects of data collection and preparation, which form the foundation for any successful AI application.

5.1. Importance of Data Collection

Overview

Data collection is the process of gathering raw information from various sources that an AI system uses to learn and make decisions. In the context of agentic AI, data is essential because it serves as the basis for training models, evaluating performance, and enabling systems to adapt to new scenarios.

Key Reasons for Data Collection:

- **Training Models:**
  AI systems learn patterns and relationships from data. The more high-quality data available, the better a model can understand complex patterns and generalize to new situations.
- **Improving Accuracy:**
  A larger and more diverse dataset helps in reducing errors and biases. It enables the system to cover a wide range of scenarios and improves prediction accuracy.
- **Enabling Adaptability:**
  Continuous data collection allows the AI system to learn from new experiences. This is particularly important for autonomous systems that operate in dynamic environments.
- **Real-World Validation:**
  Collected data from real-world sources can be used to validate and test AI models, ensuring that they perform well under various conditions.

Sources of Data

Data for agentic AI can come from various sources, including:

- **Sensor Data:**
  Information gathered from cameras, microphones, LIDAR, temperature sensors, etc.

- **User Interaction Data:**
  Logs and records of how users interact with a system (e.g., clickstreams, usage patterns).
- **Public Datasets:**
  Open-source datasets available for research, such as ImageNet for image recognition or UCI Machine Learning Repository datasets.
- **Enterprise Data:**
  Data generated within organizations, such as customer data, transaction logs, and operational metrics.

Table: Key Aspects of Data Collection

Aspect	Description	Example
Volume	The amount of data collected. More data often leads to better model performance.	Millions of images for training a computer vision model.
Variety	Diversity of data types and sources to capture different scenarios.	Sensor data, text, audio, video, and user logs.
Velocity	The speed at which data is generated and collected, important for real-time applications.	Continuous data streams from IoT devices.
Veracity	The quality and reliability of data; ensuring data is accurate and unbiased.	Data cleansing processes to remove noise or errors.

Why Data Quality Matters

The quality of the data collected directly affects the performance of an AI system. Poor-quality data may lead to inaccurate predictions or biased outcomes. It is essential to implement robust data collection methods and validation techniques to ensure that the data used is both accurate and representative.

5.2. Data Preprocessing and Feature Engineering

Overview

Once data is collected, it must be prepared for use in AI models. Data preprocessing and feature engineering are critical steps that convert raw data into a form that is more suitable for analysis. These steps improve the quality of the input data, enabling better model performance and more accurate decision-making.

Steps in Data Preprocessing:

1. **Data Cleaning:**
   Removing errors, duplicates, and inconsistencies in the dataset.
2. **Data Transformation:**
   Converting data into a uniform format. This may involve normalization, scaling, or encoding categorical variables.
3. **Handling Missing Data:**
   Addressing gaps in the data by imputation, removal, or other techniques.
4. **Data Reduction:**
   Simplifying data by reducing dimensionality, which can help in speeding up model training and reducing noise.

Feature Engineering

Feature engineering is the process of selecting, modifying, or creating new variables (features) from raw data to improve model performance. Effective feature engineering can help reveal the underlying patterns in the data, making it easier for the AI model to learn and make accurate predictions.

Key Aspects of Feature Engineering:

Aspect	Description	Example

Feature Selection	Choosing the most relevant variables that contribute to the predictive power.	Selecting only sensor measurements that directly affect system behavior.
Feature Transformation	Converting raw data into meaningful representations, such as normalization.	Scaling numerical features to a common range (e.g., 0 to 1).
Feature Creation	Deriving new features that capture additional information from the existing data.	Creating a "speed" feature from distance and time measurements.

Example: Data Preprocessing and Feature Engineering in Python

Below is a complete Python code example demonstrating data preprocessing and feature engineering using the popular libraries pandas and scikit-learn. This example uses a sample dataset to illustrate cleaning, transforming, and preparing data for a machine learning model.

python

```python
import pandas as pd

from sklearn.model_selection import train_test_split

from sklearn.preprocessing import StandardScaler, OneHotEncoder

from sklearn.impute import SimpleImputer

from sklearn.compose import ColumnTransformer

from sklearn.pipeline import Pipeline
```

```python
# Sample dataset: Simulated sensor data with some missing values and
categorical features

data = {

    'temperature': [22.5, 21.0, None, 23.1, 22.0, 21.5],

    'humidity': [45, 50, 55, None, 50, 48],

    'sensor_status': ['ok', 'ok', 'faulty', 'ok', 'faulty', 'ok'],

    'target': [1, 0, 1, 0, 1, 0]  # Binary target variable for classification

}

df = pd.DataFrame(data)

print("Original Data:")

print(df)


# Define preprocessing steps for numerical features

numeric_features = ['temperature', 'humidity']

numeric_transformer = Pipeline(steps=[

    ('imputer', SimpleImputer(strategy='mean')),   # Handle missing values

    ('scaler', StandardScaler())                # Scale features

])


# Define preprocessing steps for categorical features

categorical_features = ['sensor_status']

categorical_transformer = Pipeline(steps=[

    ('imputer', SimpleImputer(strategy='most_frequent')),  # Handle missing
values
```

```python
    ('encoder', OneHotEncoder(handle_unknown='ignore'))     # One-hot
encode categorical data

])


# Combine preprocessing steps using ColumnTransformer

preprocessor = ColumnTransformer(transformers=[

    ('num', numeric_transformer, numeric_features),

    ('cat', categorical_transformer, categorical_features)

])


# Separate features and target variable

X = df.drop('target', axis=1)

y = df['target']


# Apply the preprocessing pipeline

X_preprocessed = preprocessor.fit_transform(X)

print("\nPreprocessed Features:")

print(X_preprocessed)


# Explanation:

# - The numeric_transformer fills missing temperature and humidity
values with the mean of the column,

#   then scales the features so that they have a mean of 0 and a standard
deviation of 1.
```

```
# - The categorical_transformer fills missing sensor_status values with the
most frequent category,

#   then converts the text labels into one-hot encoded vectors.

# - The ColumnTransformer combines these steps so that numerical and
categorical features are processed appropriately.
```

Explanation of the Code:

- **Data Cleaning:**
  The SimpleImputer is used to handle missing values in both numerical (using the mean) and categorical (using the most frequent value) features.
- **Data Transformation:**
  The StandardScaler normalizes numerical data, ensuring that features like temperature and humidity are on a comparable scale. The OneHotEncoder transforms categorical data (sensor_status) into binary vectors.
- **ColumnTransformer:**
  This utility applies the appropriate preprocessing steps to the corresponding columns, simplifying the workflow for preparing data.
- **Output:**
  The processed data is printed, demonstrating how raw inputs are transformed into a format suitable for machine learning models.

Summary

- **Importance of Data Collection:**
  Data is essential for training, accuracy, adaptability, and real-world validation of agentic AI systems. A well-structured data collection process ensures that the system receives diverse, high-quality inputs.
- **Data Preprocessing and Feature Engineering:**
  Before data can be used effectively, it must be cleaned, transformed, and enhanced through feature engineering. These steps significantly impact the performance and reliability of AI models.

5.3. Model Training, Validation, and Evaluation

Once data has been collected, cleaned, and preprocessed, the next critical steps involve teaching your AI system to learn from that data, tuning it for optimal performance, and finally assessing how well it performs. These steps are divided into model training, validation, and evaluation.

Model Training

Definition:
Model training is the process in which a learning algorithm adjusts its internal parameters based on input data in order to minimize a defined loss function. During this process, the model learns to map inputs to the correct outputs.

Key Steps in Training:

1. **Data Splitting:**
    The dataset is divided into:
    - **Training Set:** The portion of data used to train the model.
    - **Validation Set:** A subset used to tune hyperparameters and prevent overfitting.
    - **Test Set:** A reserved portion used for the final evaluation of the model's performance.
2. **Learning Algorithm:**
    The algorithm iteratively adjusts weights or parameters using methods such as gradient descent to minimize errors between predictions and actual outcomes.
3. **Hyperparameter Tuning:**
    Hyperparameters (e.g., learning rate, batch size, number of epochs) are set before training and optimized based on validation performance.

Example Code for Model Training (Using Keras and the Iris Dataset):

python

```python
import numpy as np

from sklearn.datasets import load_iris

from sklearn.model_selection import train_test_split

from sklearn.preprocessing import OneHotEncoder, StandardScaler

from tensorflow.keras.models import Sequential

from tensorflow.keras.layers import Dense
```

```python
from tensorflow.keras.optimizers import Adam


# Load the Iris dataset
iris = load_iris()
X = iris.data  # Features
y = iris.target.reshape(-1, 1)  # Labels need reshaping for encoding


# One-hot encode the target variable
encoder = OneHotEncoder(sparse=False)
y_encoded = encoder.fit_transform(y)


# Standardize the features
scaler = StandardScaler()
X_scaled = scaler.fit_transform(X)


# Split data: 70% training, 15% validation, 15% testing
X_train_val, X_test, y_train_val, y_test = train_test_split(X_scaled,
y_encoded, test_size=0.15, random_state=42)

X_train, X_val, y_train, y_val = train_test_split(X_train_val, y_train_val,
test_size=0.1765, random_state=42)  # 0.1765*0.85 ~15%


# Define a simple neural network model
model = Sequential([
    Dense(10, activation='relu', input_shape=(X_train.shape[1],)),
```

```python
    Dense(10, activation='relu'),

    Dense(y_train.shape[1], activation='softmax')  # Output layer for multi-class classification

])


# Compile the model with Adam optimizer and categorical crossentropy loss

model.compile(optimizer=Adam(learning_rate=0.01), loss='categorical_crossentropy', metrics=['accuracy'])


# Train the model

history = model.fit(X_train, y_train, epochs=50, batch_size=5, validation_data=(X_val, y_val), verbose=1)


# Evaluate the model on the test set

test_loss, test_accuracy = model.evaluate(X_test, y_test, verbose=0)

print(f"Test Loss: {test_loss:.2f}, Test Accuracy: {test_accuracy:.2f}")
```

Explanation of the Code:

- **Data Splitting:**
  The dataset is divided into training, validation, and test sets. The validation set is used during training to monitor performance and avoid overfitting.
- **Model Architecture:**
  A simple feed-forward neural network is defined with two hidden layers using ReLU activations and an output layer with softmax activation, suitable for multi-class classification.
- **Compilation and Training:**
  The model is compiled with the Adam optimizer and trained using the categorical crossentropy loss function. Training progress is monitored on the validation set.

- **Evaluation:**
  Finally, the model's performance is evaluated on the test set to ensure that it generalizes well to unseen data.

Model Validation and Evaluation

Validation:
Validation involves monitoring the model's performance on a subset of data not used during training. The aim is to tune hyperparameters and adjust the model to avoid overfitting. Metrics such as validation loss and accuracy are tracked across epochs.

Evaluation:
After training, the final model is evaluated on a separate test set. Evaluation metrics may include accuracy, precision, recall, F1-score, and others depending on the problem context.

Table: Data Splitting Overview

Set	Purpose	Percentage of Total Data
Training Set	Used to adjust the model's weights	~70%
Validation Set	Used to tune hyperparameters and avoid overfitting	~15%
Test Set	Used for final evaluation of model performance	~15%

5.4. Ethics, Bias Mitigation, and Data Integrity

As AI systems are deployed in increasingly critical applications, ethical considerations, bias mitigation, and data integrity become paramount. This section covers why these factors are essential and how to address them in the context of agentic AI.

Ethical Considerations in AI

Overview:
Ethical AI involves ensuring that systems operate fairly, transparently, and in ways that respect user privacy and societal values. Key ethical principles include:

- **Fairness:**
  The system should treat all groups equitably without favoring or discriminating against any subset of users.
- **Transparency:**
  AI systems should be explainable, and their decision-making processes should be understandable to stakeholders.
- **Privacy:**
  User data must be handled securely, and the collection, storage, and processing of data must comply with legal standards and ethical guidelines.

Bias Mitigation

Sources of Bias:
Bias in AI can arise from various sources:

- **Historical Bias:**
  Data that reflects historical inequities.
- **Sampling Bias:**
  Non-representative data that does not capture the diversity of the target population.
- **Algorithmic Bias:**
  Bias introduced by the design of the model or decision-making processes.

Techniques to Mitigate Bias:

Technique	Description	Example

Data Augmentation:	Enhancing the dataset to better represent diverse groups.	Oversampling minority classes in a dataset.
Fairness Constraints:	Incorporating fairness metrics into the training process to balance outcomes.	Adding penalty terms for unequal error rates across groups.
Regular Auditing:	Continuously monitoring and evaluating models for signs of bias.	Periodic audits of model predictions and error analysis.
Explainability Tools:	Using techniques like SHAP or LIME to understand model decisions.	Visualizing feature importance to ensure decisions are reasonable.

Data Integrity

Overview:
Data integrity refers to maintaining the accuracy, consistency, and reliability of data throughout its lifecycle. High data integrity is crucial because:

- **Model Performance:**
  Garbage in, garbage out—poor data quality can severely hamper the performance of AI models.
- **Trust and Transparency:**
  Reliable data underpins trust in AI systems, especially in sensitive applications.

Steps to Ensure Data Integrity:

1. **Data Validation:**
   Implement automated checks during data collection and preprocessing to detect anomalies or errors.

2. **Version Control:**
   Use version control systems for datasets to track changes and ensure consistency over time.
3. **Security Measures:**
   Protect data through encryption, access control, and secure storage practices to prevent unauthorized modifications.
4. **Documentation:**
   Maintain clear documentation about data sources, preprocessing steps, and any changes made to the data.

Example: Bias Mitigation in Preprocessing

Below is a simple Python snippet demonstrating a bias mitigation strategy during data preprocessing. In this example, we use oversampling to balance classes in a dataset.

python

```python
import pandas as pd

from sklearn.utils import resample


# Simulated dataset with imbalanced classes
data = {

    'feature1': [1.2, 2.3, 1.9, 3.4, 2.1, 1.8, 3.0, 2.5],

    'feature2': [0.5, 1.1, 0.7, 1.3, 0.9, 0.6, 1.0, 1.2],

    'class':   ['A', 'A', 'A', 'B', 'B', 'B', 'B', 'B']  # Class A is underrepresented

}

df = pd.DataFrame(data)


print("Original Class Distribution:")

print(df['class'].value_counts())
```

```python
# Separate majority and minority classes

df_majority = df[df['class'] == 'B']

df_minority = df[df['class'] == 'A']


# Upsample minority class

df_minority_upsampled = resample(df_minority,

                replace=True,       # sample with replacement

                n_samples=len(df_majority),  # match majority class count

                random_state=42)      # for reproducibility


# Combine majority class with upsampled minority class

df_balanced = pd.concat([df_majority, df_minority_upsampled])


print("\nBalanced Class Distribution:")

print(df_balanced['class'].value_counts())
```

Explanation of the Code:

- **Initial Dataset:**
  The dataset is simulated with an imbalance between classes 'A' and 'B'.
- **Resampling:**
  The resample function from scikit-learn is used to oversample the minority class ('A') so that it matches the count of the majority class ('B').
- **Outcome:**
  The resulting DataFrame, df_balanced, has a balanced class distribution, which is an important step in mitigating bias before model training.

Summary

- **Model Training, Validation, and Evaluation:**
  This process involves splitting data into training, validation, and test sets, using learning algorithms to adjust model parameters, and fine-tuning the model based on validation performance. A complete code example illustrates how to train a neural network model using the Iris dataset.
- **Ethics, Bias Mitigation, and Data Integrity:**
  Ensuring that AI systems are ethical and fair involves addressing bias at multiple stages—from data collection and preprocessing to model evaluation. Data integrity practices such as validation, version control, and security measures are vital to building trustworthy AI systems. Techniques like data augmentation and oversampling help mitigate bias, as shown in the provided code example.

Together, these sections underscore the importance of rigorous model development practices and ethical considerations in creating robust, reliable, and fair agentic AI systems.

5.5. Hands-On Exercise: Cleaning and Preparing a Dataset

In this exercise, you will learn how to transform a raw dataset into a clean and well-prepared format for further analysis or machine learning. The process includes handling missing values, removing duplicates, converting data types, and applying feature scaling or encoding as needed.

Step 1: Understanding the Dataset

For demonstration purposes, let's assume we have a simple dataset collected from sensors. The dataset contains readings for temperature, humidity, and a sensor status, along with a target variable. Some values are missing or inconsistent, and the sensor status is given as categorical data.

Below is a table summarizing our sample dataset:

Column Name	Description	Data Type	Issues

temperature	Temperature reading in degrees Celsius	Numeric (float)	Some missing values
humidity	Humidity percentage	Numeric (int)	Some missing values
sensor_status	Status of the sensor ("ok", "faulty")	Categorical	May contain missing or inconsistent entries
target	Binary target variable for classification (0 or 1)	Numeric (int)	Clean

Step 2: Importing Libraries and Creating the Dataset

We begin by importing the necessary libraries and creating our sample dataset.

python

```python
import pandas as pd

import numpy as np


# Create a sample dataset

data = {

    'temperature': [22.5, 21.0, np.nan, 23.1, 22.0, 21.5],

    'humidity': [45, 50, 55, np.nan, 50, 48],
```

```python
    'sensor_status': ['ok', 'ok', 'faulty', 'ok', 'faulty', None],

    'target': [1, 0, 1, 0, 1, 0]

}


df = pd.DataFrame(data)

print("Original Data:")

print(df)
```

Explanation:

- We use pandas to create a DataFrame from a dictionary.
- numpy.nan is used to simulate missing values in the numeric columns.
- The original dataset is printed for initial inspection.

Step 3: Data Cleaning

A. Handling Missing Values
Missing values can be addressed by imputation (filling in missing values) or by removing the affected rows or columns. In this example, we will fill missing numeric values with the column mean and categorical values with the most frequent value.

python

```python
from sklearn.impute import SimpleImputer


# Create imputer for numeric features: fill missing values with the mean

numeric_imputer = SimpleImputer(strategy='mean')


# Apply imputer on numeric columns: 'temperature' and 'humidity'
```

```python
df[['temperature', 'humidity']] =
numeric_imputer.fit_transform(df[['temperature', 'humidity']])


# For categorical features, fill missing values with the most frequent
category

categorical_imputer = SimpleImputer(strategy='most_frequent')

df[['sensor_status']] =
categorical_imputer.fit_transform(df[['sensor_status']])


print("\nData after handling missing values:")

print(df)
```

Explanation:

- We use SimpleImputer from scikit-learn with a strategy of 'mean' for numeric columns.
- For categorical data (sensor_status), the strategy 'most_frequent' fills in missing entries with the most common value.
- The cleaned dataset is printed to verify that missing values are handled.

B. Removing Duplicates
Duplicates can skew model training. Check and remove any duplicate rows if present.

python

```python
# Check for duplicates

duplicates = df.duplicated()

print("\nDuplicates in the dataset:")

print(duplicates)
```

```python
# Remove duplicates (if any)

df = df.drop_duplicates()

print("\nData after removing duplicates:")

print(df)
```

Explanation:

- The duplicated() function identifies duplicate rows.
- The drop_duplicates() function removes any duplicates found.
- The dataset is printed again to ensure no duplicate rows remain.

Step 4: Data Transformation and Feature Engineering

A. Converting Data Types
Ensure that each column has the appropriate data type for processing. For instance, converting sensor_status to a categorical type may help in encoding.

python

```python
# Convert sensor_status to a categorical type

df['sensor_status'] = df['sensor_status'].astype('category')

print("\nData types after conversion:")

print(df.dtypes)
```

B. Feature Scaling and Encoding
Scale numeric features and encode categorical features. Here, we use scikit-learn's StandardScaler for numeric scaling and OneHotEncoder for encoding categorical variables.

python

```python
from sklearn.preprocessing import StandardScaler, OneHotEncoder
from sklearn.compose import ColumnTransformer
from sklearn.pipeline import Pipeline


# Define preprocessing steps for numeric features
numeric_features = ['temperature', 'humidity']
numeric_transformer = Pipeline(steps=[
    ('scaler', StandardScaler())
])


# Define preprocessing steps for categorical features
categorical_features = ['sensor_status']
categorical_transformer = Pipeline(steps=[
    ('encoder', OneHotEncoder(handle_unknown='ignore'))
])


# Combine preprocessing using ColumnTransformer
preprocessor = ColumnTransformer(transformers=[
    ('num', numeric_transformer, numeric_features),
    ('cat', categorical_transformer, categorical_features)
])


# Apply the transformations
```

```
X = df.drop('target', axis=1)

y = df['target']


X_preprocessed = preprocessor.fit_transform(X)

print("\nPreprocessed Features (after scaling and encoding):")

print(X_preprocessed)
```

Explanation:

- **Numeric Transformation:**
  We use StandardScaler to standardize the numeric features to have a mean of 0 and a standard deviation of 1.
- **Categorical Transformation:**
  We use OneHotEncoder to convert the sensor_status column into a binary matrix.
- **ColumnTransformer:**
  This tool applies different transformations to specified columns and combines the results.
- The preprocessed features are printed as a NumPy array.

Step 5: Summary of the Data Cleaning Process

The following table summarizes the main tasks performed in cleaning and preparing the dataset:

Step	Purpose	Method/Tool
Initial Inspection	Understand raw data and identify issues	Pandas DataFrame, df.head()

Handling Missing Values	Fill or remove missing entries	SimpleImputer with strategies 'mean' and 'most_frequent'
Removing Duplicates	Eliminate duplicate rows to prevent bias	drop_duplicates()
Data Type Conversion	Ensure each column has the correct type	Pandas .astype() method
Feature Scaling	Standardize numeric features for consistency	StandardScaler
Encoding Categorical Data	Convert text categories into numerical format	OneHotEncoder
Combining Transformations	Apply multiple preprocessing steps to the dataset	ColumnTransformer

This hands-on exercise has demonstrated how to clean and prepare a dataset for machine learning. By following these steps—inspecting data, handling missing values, removing duplicates, converting data types, and performing feature scaling and encoding—you ensure that the dataset is in optimal condition for model training and evaluation. The provided Python code examples illustrate each step in a practical, reproducible manner, making the process accessible to beginners and professionals alike.

Chapter 6 Developing Your Own Agentic AI System

Building an agentic AI system begins with setting up the right development environment and choosing the appropriate tools and platforms. In this section, we explain how to prepare your system for AI development and provide an overview of popular frameworks such as TensorFlow and PyTorch.

6.1. Setting Up Your Development Environment

A well-configured development environment is essential for efficiently building, testing, and deploying AI applications. The setup involves installing necessary software, libraries, and tools, along with establishing a clear workflow.

Steps to Set Up Your Environment

1. **Choose Your Operating System:**
   ○ Most AI development work is done on Linux, macOS, or Windows. Linux (e.g., Ubuntu) is popular because of its robust support for development tools and ease of installing dependencies.
2. **Install Python:**
   ○ Python is the de facto language for AI development. Download and install the latest version of Python (preferably 3.7 or later).

Verify the installation by running:
bash

```
python --version
```

   ○

3. **Set Up a Virtual Environment:**
   ○ Virtual environments help manage dependencies and avoid conflicts between projects.

Create a virtual environment using venv or conda. For example, using venv:
bash

```
python -m venv agentic_ai_env
```

```bash
source agentic_ai_env/bin/activate  # On Windows:
agentic_ai_env\Scripts\activate
```

4. **Install Essential Libraries:**

Install common libraries for data manipulation, visualization, and AI model development. For instance:
bash

```bash
pip install numpy pandas matplotlib scikit-learn
```

5. **Set Up an IDE or Code Editor:**
   ○ Popular choices include Visual Studio Code, PyCharm, or Jupyter Notebook. These tools offer features like syntax highlighting, debugging, and integrated terminals.

For interactive development and visualization, Jupyter Notebook is an excellent choice. Install it via:
bash

```bash
pip install jupyter
```

Example: Creating a Virtual Environment and Installing Packages

Below is a complete shell script example to set up your environment on a Unix-based system:

bash

```bash
#!/bin/bash

# Step 1: Check Python version

echo "Python Version:"
```

```
python --version


# Step 2: Create a virtual environment named 'agentic_ai_env'

echo "Creating virtual environment..."

python -m venv agentic_ai_env


# Step 3: Activate the virtual environment

echo "Activating virtual environment..."

source agentic_ai_env/bin/activate


# Step 4: Upgrade pip and install essential libraries

echo "Upgrading pip and installing packages..."

pip install --upgrade pip

pip install numpy pandas matplotlib scikit-learn jupyter


echo "Environment setup complete. To start Jupyter Notebook, run 'jupyter notebook'."
```

Explanation:

- The script checks the Python version, creates a virtual environment, activates it, upgrades pip, and installs essential libraries.
- This script ensures that your environment is isolated and prepared for building AI models.

Recommended Development Workflow

- **Version Control:**
  Use Git for tracking changes and collaborating with others. Set up a GitHub repository to store your project code.
- **Notebook vs. Script:**
  Use Jupyter Notebooks for exploratory data analysis and quick prototyping, and Python scripts or modules for production code.
- **Documentation:**
  Keep detailed notes and documentation (using Markdown files or inline comments) to explain code functionality and project structure.

6.2. Overview of Tools and Platforms (TensorFlow, PyTorch, etc.)

Choosing the right tools and platforms is critical for developing and deploying agentic AI systems. Two of the most widely used frameworks in AI are TensorFlow and PyTorch.

TensorFlow

Overview:

- **Developer:** Google Brain Team
- **Strengths:**
  - Mature ecosystem with robust support for production environments.
  - Extensive documentation and community resources.
  - Supports both high-level Keras API for ease of use and low-level API for advanced customization.
- **Use Cases:**
  - Deep learning applications, such as image and speech recognition.
  - Scalable deployment in cloud and edge environments.

Key Features:

Feature	Description
Keras API	High-level, user-friendly interface for building models.

TensorBoard	Tool for visualizing model training and performance.
TPU Support	Optimized for high-performance hardware in the cloud.

Example: Simple Neural Network with TensorFlow/Keras

python

```python
import tensorflow as tf

from tensorflow.keras.models import Sequential

from tensorflow.keras.layers import Dense

from sklearn.datasets import load_iris

from sklearn.model_selection import train_test_split

from sklearn.preprocessing import StandardScaler, OneHotEncoder

import numpy as np


# Load and preprocess the Iris dataset

iris = load_iris()

X = iris.data

y = iris.target.reshape(-1, 1)


# One-hot encode the target variable

encoder = OneHotEncoder(sparse=False)
```

```python
y_encoded = encoder.fit_transform(y)


# Standardize the features

scaler = StandardScaler()

X_scaled = scaler.fit_transform(X)


# Split the dataset

X_train, X_test, y_train, y_test = train_test_split(X_scaled, y_encoded,
test_size=0.2, random_state=42)


# Define a simple neural network model using Keras

model = Sequential([

    Dense(10, activation='relu', input_shape=(X_train.shape[1],)),

    Dense(10, activation='relu'),

    Dense(y_encoded.shape[1], activation='softmax')

])


# Compile the model

model.compile(optimizer='adam', loss='categorical_crossentropy',
metrics=['accuracy'])


# Train the model

model.fit(X_train, y_train, epochs=50, batch_size=5, validation_split=0.1)
```

```python
# Evaluate the model

loss, accuracy = model.evaluate(X_test, y_test)

print(f"Test Accuracy: {accuracy:.2f}")
```

Explanation:

- The code loads the Iris dataset, preprocesses it (scaling and encoding), and builds a simple neural network model using TensorFlow/Keras.
- The model is compiled with the Adam optimizer and trained for 50 epochs.
- Finally, the model's accuracy on the test set is printed.

PyTorch

Overview:

- **Developer:** Facebook's AI Research Lab (FAIR)
- **Strengths:**
  - Dynamic computation graph that makes it intuitive and flexible for research.
  - Preferred for rapid prototyping and experimentation.
  - Strong community support and extensive ecosystem (e.g., TorchVision for image processing).
- **Use Cases:**
  - Research applications, experimental models, and projects that require dynamic changes in the model architecture.

Key Features:

Feature	Description
Dynamic Computation Graph	Allows changes to the graph on-the-fly, making debugging easier.
Extensive Libraries	Ecosystem includes libraries like TorchVision and TorchText.

| Community Support | Strong and active research community with frequent updates. |

Example: Simple Neural Network with PyTorch

python

```python
import torch
import torch.nn as nn
import torch.optim as optim
from sklearn.datasets import load_iris
from sklearn.model_selection import train_test_split
from sklearn.preprocessing import StandardScaler, OneHotEncoder
import numpy as np

# Load and preprocess the Iris dataset
iris = load_iris()
X = iris.data
y = iris.target.reshape(-1, 1)

# One-hot encode the target variable
encoder = OneHotEncoder(sparse=False)
y_encoded = encoder.fit_transform(y)

# Standardize the features
```

```python
scaler = StandardScaler()

X_scaled = scaler.fit_transform(X)


# Convert data to torch tensors

X_tensor = torch.tensor(X_scaled, dtype=torch.float32)

y_tensor = torch.tensor(np.argmax(y_encoded, axis=1), dtype=torch.long)


# Split the dataset into training and test sets

train_size = int(0.8 * len(X_tensor))

X_train, X_test = X_tensor[:train_size], X_tensor[train_size:]

y_train, y_test = y_tensor[:train_size], y_tensor[train_size:]


# Define a simple neural network model using PyTorch

class SimpleNN(nn.Module):

    def __init__(self, input_dim, hidden_dim, output_dim):

        super(SimpleNN, self).__init__()

        self.fc1 = nn.Linear(input_dim, hidden_dim)

        self.relu = nn.ReLU()

        self.fc2 = nn.Linear(hidden_dim, hidden_dim)

        self.fc3 = nn.Linear(hidden_dim, output_dim)


    def forward(self, x):

        out = self.fc1(x)
```

```python
        out = self.relu(out)

        out = self.fc2(out)

        out = self.relu(out)

        out = self.fc3(out)

        return out


input_dim = X_train.shape[1]

hidden_dim = 10

output_dim = y_encoded.shape[1]


model = SimpleNN(input_dim, hidden_dim, output_dim)


# Define loss function and optimizer

criterion = nn.CrossEntropyLoss()

optimizer = optim.Adam(model.parameters(), lr=0.01)


# Training loop

epochs = 50

for epoch in range(epochs):

    model.train()

    optimizer.zero_grad()

    outputs = model(X_train)

    loss = criterion(outputs, y_train)
```

```python
loss.backward()

optimizer.step()


if (epoch+1) % 10 == 0:

    print(f"Epoch [{epoch+1}/{epochs}], Loss: {loss.item():.4f}")


# Evaluate the model

model.eval()

with torch.no_grad():

    outputs = model(X_test)

    _, predicted = torch.max(outputs.data, 1)

    accuracy = (predicted == y_test).sum().item() / len(y_test)

    print(f"Test Accuracy: {accuracy:.2f}")
```

Explanation:

- The code loads and preprocesses the Iris dataset, converting it into PyTorch tensors.
- A simple neural network model is defined using the PyTorch nn.Module class.
- The model is trained using a standard training loop with the Adam optimizer and cross-entropy loss.
- After training, the model's performance is evaluated on the test set, and the accuracy is printed.

Summary

- **Setting Up Your Development Environment:**
    - Choose an operating system, install Python, set up a virtual environment, and install essential libraries.

o Use tools such as Git for version control and an IDE or Jupyter Notebook for coding.
- **Overview of Tools and Platforms:**
  o **TensorFlow:**
    ▪ Ideal for production environments, offers the high-level Keras API, and provides tools like TensorBoard.
  o **PyTorch:**
    ▪ Preferred for research and rapid prototyping due to its dynamic computation graph and flexibility.

These steps and tools create a solid foundation for developing your own agentic AI system, enabling you to efficiently design, train, and deploy intelligent autonomous systems.

6.3. Step-by-Step: Building a Simple Autonomous Agent

In this section, we will create a basic autonomous agent that operates in a simplified environment. The agent's goal is to move toward a target position using simple decision-making based on sensor input. We will build the agent in Python and explain each step in detail.

Step 1: Define the Problem

Imagine an environment where the agent starts at a given position on a one-dimensional line. Its objective is to reach a target position. The agent perceives its distance from the target (with some noise) and decides whether to move right, move left, or stay in place.

Step 2: Outline the Agent's Components

An autonomous agent generally comprises:

- **Perception:** Collecting sensor input to measure the difference between the current position and the target.
- **Decision-Making:** Evaluating the sensor input to decide which action to take.
- **Action:** Executing the chosen action to update the position.
- **Feedback Loop:** Receiving updated sensor input after acting to continuously adjust behavior.

Step 3: Implement the Agent in Python

Below is a complete Python code example that puts these components together.

python

```python
import random

class SimpleAutonomousAgent:
    def __init__(self, target_position):
        self.position = 0          # Starting position
        self.target = target_position  # Target the agent must reach
        self.memory = []           # To store recent sensor inputs (optional for adaptation)

    def perceive(self):
        """
        Simulate the sensor reading by calculating the difference between
        the current position and the target position, with added random noise.
        """
        # Calculate error with noise to simulate sensor imperfections.
        error = (self.target - self.position) + random.uniform(-0.2, 0.2)
        self.memory.append(error)
        print(f"Perception: Sensor error = {error:.2f}")
        return error

    def decide(self, error):
        """
```

```python
        Decide which action to take based on the sensor error.

        A simple heuristic:
          - If error > 0, move right.
          - If error < 0, move left.
          - If error is close to zero, hold position.
        """

        if error > 0.1:
            decision = "Move Right"
        elif error < -0.1:
            decision = "Move Left"
        else:
            decision = "Hold Position"
        print(f"Decision: {decision}")
        return decision


    def act(self, decision):
        """
        Execute the action based on the decision.
        """
        if decision == "Move Right":
            self.position += 1
        elif decision == "Move Left":
            self.position -= 1
```

```python
        # No change if holding position.
        print(f"Actuation: New position = {self.position}")


    def run(self, steps=10):
        """
        Run the agent's decision loop for a specified number of steps.
        """
        print(f"Starting Autonomous Agent. Target Position = {self.target}")
        for step in range(steps):
            print(f"\n--- Step {step + 1} ---")
            error = self.perceive()
            decision = self.decide(error)
            self.act(decision)
            # Provide immediate feedback by checking new error
            current_error = self.target - self.position
            print(f"Feedback: Current error = {current_error:.2f}")
            # Optionally break early if target is reached
            if abs(current_error) < 0.1:
                print("Target reached!")
                break
        print("Decision loop completed.")


# Example usage:
```

```
if __name__ == "__main__":

    agent = SimpleAutonomousAgent(target_position=5)

    agent.run(steps=15)
```

Explanation of the Code

1. **Initialization:**
   - The SimpleAutonomousAgent class is initialized with a target position and a starting position of 0.
   - A memory list is included to optionally store past sensor readings.
2. **Perception:**
   - The perceive method computes the error (difference between target and current position) and adds random noise to simulate real-world sensor variability.
   - The sensor reading is printed and stored in memory.
3. **Decision-Making:**
   - The decide method uses a simple heuristic:
     - If the error is greater than 0.1, the agent moves right.
     - If less than -0.1, it moves left.
     - Otherwise, it holds its position.
   - The decision is printed.
4. **Action:**
   - The act method updates the agent's position based on the decision.
   - The new position is printed.
5. **Feedback Loop:**
   - After each action, the agent receives feedback by computing the new error.
   - The loop runs for a fixed number of steps or stops early if the target is reached.

6.4. Best Practices, Common Pitfalls, and Learning Outcomes

Best Practices

Implementing an autonomous agent involves many design choices. Here are some best practices:

- **Modular Design:**
  Separate the perception, decision-making, and actuation processes into distinct functions or classes. This makes the code easier to test and maintain.
- **Incremental Development:**
  Build and test each component separately before integrating them. For example, test the perception module with simulated data before adding decision logic.
- **Robust Error Handling:**
  Include mechanisms to handle unexpected sensor inputs or other runtime errors gracefully.
- **Logging and Visualization:**
  Print or log the agent's decisions and state changes. Use visualizations (like graphs or flowcharts) to monitor the agent's behavior over time.
- **Documentation:**
  Comment your code and provide clear documentation for each module. This is especially important in research or collaborative projects.
- **Parameter Tuning:**
  Experiment with different thresholds in your decision logic (e.g., the error margin for "Hold Position") to optimize performance in different scenarios.

Common Pitfalls

- **Overfitting to Simplistic Scenarios:**
  If the simulation environment is too simple, the agent may perform well in simulation but fail in more complex real-world situations.
- **Ignoring Sensor Noise:**
  Real-world sensors introduce noise; if your agent's decision-making doesn't account for this, it can lead to erratic behavior.
- **Poor Feedback Loop:**
  Failing to incorporate a robust feedback mechanism may prevent the agent from learning effectively from its actions.
- **Lack of Modularity:**
  Writing monolithic code can lead to difficulties in debugging and future modifications.

Learning Outcomes

By completing this section, you will have mastered the following:

Learning Outcome	Description

Understand Agent Architecture	Learn how to divide an agent's functionality into perception, decision-making, and actuation.
Implement a Decision Loop	Build a loop that continuously perceives, decides, acts, and receives feedback.
Work with Simple Heuristics	Use basic rules to decide actions, a foundation that can later be replaced with more complex models.
Integrate and Test Components	Gain experience in modular development by testing each component independently before integration.
Identify and Avoid Common Pitfalls	Recognize common issues in autonomous agent design and learn strategies to mitigate them.

Summary

- **Step-by-Step Implementation:**
  We built a simple autonomous agent that reads sensor inputs, makes decisions using a basic heuristic, acts to update its position, and receives feedback—all integrated into a continuous loop.
- **Best Practices and Pitfalls:**
  We discussed design best practices, including modularity, robust error handling, and incremental development, as well as common pitfalls like overfitting and ignoring sensor noise.
- **Learning Outcomes:**
  By following this guide, you will understand how to build and evaluate a simple autonomous agent, setting the stage for more advanced projects in agentic AI.

Chapter 7 Practical Applications of Agentic AI

Agentic AI is transforming multiple sectors by automating decision-making processes, optimizing operations, and creating new user experiences. This section explores how agentic AI is being applied in business and industry, as well as in consumer-focused applications.

7.1. Agentic AI in Business and Industry

Overview

In business and industrial settings, agentic AI systems are designed to improve efficiency, reduce costs, and drive innovation. They enable companies to automate repetitive tasks, make data-driven decisions, and respond in real time to changing market conditions.

Key Application Areas

1. **Autonomous Operations:**
   - **Manufacturing and Robotics:**
     Autonomous robots in assembly lines adjust their actions based on real-time sensor data, improving production efficiency and safety.
   - **Supply Chain Optimization:**
     Agentic AI monitors inventory levels, predicts demand, and automatically reorders supplies, reducing waste and ensuring smooth operations.
2. **Predictive Maintenance:**
   - **Overview:**
     AI-powered systems analyze equipment data to predict failures before they occur.
   - **Benefits:**
     Reduces downtime, extends equipment life, and minimizes maintenance costs.
3. **Financial Services:**
   - **Algorithmic Trading:**
     Autonomous systems analyze vast amounts of market data, execute trades, and adjust strategies dynamically, often faster and more accurately than human traders.
   - **Fraud Detection:**
     Continuous monitoring and pattern recognition help detect unusual transactions and potential fraud in real time.

4. **Customer Service and Support:**
   o **Chatbots and Virtual Assistants:**
     These agents can handle customer inquiries, process requests, and escalate complex issues to human operators.
   o **Personalized Marketing:**
     By analyzing customer behavior, agentic AI tailors marketing strategies to individual preferences, improving engagement and sales.

Table: Examples of Business Applications

Application Area	Description	Example
Autonomous Manufacturing	Robots adjust production in real time based on sensor data.	Automated assembly lines in automotive factories.
Supply Chain Management	AI systems optimize inventory and logistics.	Predictive reordering systems in retail supply chains.
Predictive Maintenance	Monitoring equipment to foresee and prevent breakdowns.	AI sensors on industrial machinery that schedule maintenance.
Algorithmic Trading	Real-time trading decisions using market data.	High-frequency trading systems in financial markets.
Fraud Detection	Continuous transaction analysis to flag anomalies.	AI systems in banking that detect fraudulent activities.

Customer Service	Virtual agents handling inquiries and support tickets.	Chatbots on e-commerce websites and customer help desks.

Example: Inventory Management Simulation

The following Python code simulates a simple autonomous inventory management agent. The agent monitors stock levels and places an order if the inventory falls below a defined threshold.

python

```python
import random


class InventoryAgent:
    def __init__(self, initial_stock, reorder_threshold, reorder_amount):
        self.stock = initial_stock
        self.threshold = reorder_threshold
        self.reorder_amount = reorder_amount

    def perceive_stock(self):
        # Simulate sensor reading with a small random variation
        current_stock = self.stock + random.randint(-2, 2)
        print(f"Perceived stock level: {current_stock}")
        return current_stock

    def decide(self, current_stock):
```

```python
        if current_stock < self.threshold:
            decision = "Reorder"
        else:
            decision = "Hold"
        print(f"Decision: {decision}")
        return decision

    def act(self, decision):
        if decision == "Reorder":
            self.stock += self.reorder_amount
            print(f"Action: Reordered {self.reorder_amount} items. New stock: {self.stock}")
        else:
            print("Action: No reorder needed.")

    def run_cycle(self, cycles=5):
        print("Starting inventory management simulation...")
        for cycle in range(cycles):
            print(f"\nCycle {cycle + 1}:")
            current_stock = self.perceive_stock()
            decision = self.decide(current_stock)
            self.act(decision)
        print("Simulation complete.")
```

```
# Example usage:

if __name__ == "__main__":

    agent = InventoryAgent(initial_stock=50, reorder_threshold=45,
reorder_amount=20)

    agent.run_cycle(cycles=10)
```

Explanation:

- **Perception:**
  The perceive_stock method simulates reading the current stock level with slight variations.
- **Decision-Making:**
  The agent decides whether to reorder stock based on a predefined threshold.
- **Action:**
  If the stock is low, the agent orders additional items.
- **Cycle Execution:**
  The simulation runs multiple cycles to illustrate continuous monitoring and decision-making.

7.2. Consumer Applications and Everyday Use Cases

Overview

For consumers, agentic AI enhances daily life by automating routine tasks, providing personalized assistance, and improving the functionality of smart devices. These systems are designed to be intuitive and accessible, making advanced technology a part of everyday living.

Key Application Areas

1. **Smart Homes:**
   - **Overview:**
     AI-powered devices in smart homes manage lighting, temperature, security, and energy consumption.

- **Example:**
  A smart thermostat that learns your schedule and adjusts temperatures automatically for comfort and energy savings.

2. **Digital Assistants:**
   - **Overview:**
     Virtual assistants like Siri, Alexa, and Google Assistant use agentic AI to manage tasks, answer queries, and control smart devices.
   - **Example:**
     Voice-activated assistants that can schedule appointments, send messages, and provide real-time information.

3. **Wearable Technology:**
   - **Overview:**
     Devices like smartwatches and fitness trackers use AI to monitor health metrics, track activity, and provide personalized feedback.
   - **Example:**
     A smartwatch that detects irregular heart rates and prompts you to seek medical advice if necessary.

4. **Personalized Recommendations:**
   - **Overview:**
     Agentic AI analyzes user behavior and preferences to recommend products, media, or services tailored to individual tastes.
   - **Example:**
     Streaming services that curate playlists or suggest movies based on your viewing history.

5. **Automated Transportation:**
   - **Overview:**
     Autonomous vehicles and ride-sharing services utilize agentic AI to navigate, optimize routes, and enhance safety.
   - **Example:**
     Self-driving cars that adjust routes based on real-time traffic data.

Table: Examples of Consumer Applications

Application Area	Description	Example
Smart Homes	Devices automate home management, improving	Smart thermostats, automated lighting, security systems.

	energy efficiency and convenience.	
Digital Assistants	Virtual assistants manage tasks, control devices, and provide personalized services.	Siri, Alexa, Google Assistant.
Wearable Technology	AI-enhanced wearables monitor health and fitness, providing real-time feedback.	Smartwatches, fitness trackers, health monitors.
Personalized Recommendations	Tailors content and product suggestions based on user data and behavior.	Netflix movie recommendations, Amazon product suggestions.
Automated Transportation	Autonomous systems optimize travel routes, reduce congestion, and enhance safety.	Self-driving cars, autonomous ride-sharing services.

Consumer Use Case Example: Smart Home Thermostat

Imagine a smart thermostat that learns your daily schedule, adjusting heating and cooling automatically. Such a device uses sensor data (room temperature, occupancy, weather forecasts) to decide the optimal settings for comfort and energy savings. Agentic AI in this context involves continuous monitoring, decision-making based on user preferences and environmental conditions, and executing actions to adjust the temperature.

Conceptual Flow:

1. **Data Collection:**
   Sensors capture room temperature, occupancy data, and local weather information.

2. **Decision-Making:**
   The AI system compares current readings to user preferences and predefined comfort levels.
3. **Action:**
   The thermostat adjusts the HVAC system to achieve the desired temperature.
4. **Feedback:**
   The system monitors the changes and refines its decisions over time based on user feedback and evolving conditions.

While a complete code example for a smart thermostat would require integration with hardware and APIs, the logic mirrors the decision-making loop demonstrated in the business example. The goal is to create a seamless, self-regulating system that improves the user's daily experience.

Summary

- **Agentic AI in Business and Industry:**
  In business contexts, agentic AI is used to optimize manufacturing, supply chain management, predictive maintenance, financial trading, fraud detection, and customer service. The provided inventory management simulation exemplifies how autonomous agents can streamline operations.
- **Consumer Applications:**
  For everyday use, agentic AI powers smart homes, digital assistants, wearable devices, personalized recommendation systems, and autonomous transportation. These applications enhance convenience, safety, and personalization in daily life.

By understanding these practical applications, you gain insight into the diverse roles that agentic AI plays across industries and in personal life. Whether optimizing complex industrial processes or enhancing everyday experiences, agentic AI is a powerful tool driving innovation and efficiency in our modern world.

7.3. Startups and Disruptive Innovations

Overview

Startups and disruptive innovations play a critical role in the evolution of agentic AI. By leveraging cutting-edge technologies, small and agile companies can challenge established business models and drive rapid change across industries. These startups often focus on niche applications or novel approaches that traditional companies may overlook.

How Startups Use Agentic AI to Disrupt Markets

1. **Niche Focus and Agility:**
   - **Flexibility:** Startups are less burdened by legacy systems and can quickly adapt new technologies.
   - **Market Gaps:** They identify and target underserved areas where agentic AI can provide a significant competitive advantage.
2. **Innovative Business Models:**
   - **Automation and Efficiency:** Many startups use agentic AI to automate processes that were previously labor-intensive, leading to cost savings and increased speed.
   - **Data-Driven Insights:** Startups often build platforms that integrate real-time data analysis with autonomous decision-making, allowing them to offer personalized and scalable solutions.
3. **Collaboration and Ecosystem Building:**
   - **Partnerships:** Startups collaborate with larger companies, research institutions, and investors to accelerate development.
   - **Open-Source and Community Engagement:** Leveraging open-source AI frameworks and active developer communities helps startups iterate quickly and adopt best practices.

Examples of Disruptive Innovations Powered by Agentic AI

The table below provides examples of hypothetical startups or innovations that use agentic AI to disrupt their respective markets:

Startup/Innovation	Sector	Application of Agentic AI	Impact
AutoOptima	Supply Chain Management	Uses autonomous agents to optimize inventory and logistics in real time.	Reduces waste, cuts costs, and ensures efficient supply flow.
MedAssist AI	Healthcare	Develops intelligent diagnostic assistants that learn	Speeds up diagnosis, reduces errors, and

		from patient data to improve accuracy over time.	supports medical staff.
FinEdge	Financial Services	Implements algorithmic trading and fraud detection using continuous data analysis and adaptive decision-making.	Improves trading speed and risk management while reducing fraud.
SmartHome Nexus	Consumer Technology	Creates integrated smart home systems that learn residents' habits and adjust energy use and security measures accordingly.	Enhances home automation and reduces energy consumption.
EduAdapt	Education	Uses personalized learning agents that adapt educational content to each student's pace and learning style.	Improves engagement and learning outcomes in online education.

Case Example: Disruptive Innovation in Retail

Consider a startup that uses agentic AI to reinvent the retail shopping experience. By integrating sensor data from in-store cameras, real-time customer tracking, and predictive analytics, the startup creates an intelligent inventory management and customer engagement system. This system dynamically adjusts product placements and personalized offers based on observed shopper behavior. As a result, stores see increased sales and improved customer satisfaction, while operating costs decrease through better inventory management.

7.4. Real-World Success Stories and Interactive Case Studies

Overview

Real-world success stories and interactive case studies bring agentic AI concepts to life. They offer practical insights into how companies and organizations have implemented autonomous systems to solve real problems. Case studies not only highlight the benefits but also share lessons learned, challenges faced, and strategies for overcoming common pitfalls.

Components of an Interactive Case Study

1. **Background and Context:**
   - **Industry Overview:** Provide context about the industry or problem area.
   - **Objective:** Clearly state the goals that the agentic AI solution aimed to achieve.
2. **Implementation Details:**
   - **Technology Stack:** Describe the tools, platforms, and algorithms used.
   - **Process Flow:** Outline the key steps from data collection to decision-making and actuation.
   - **Challenges:** Discuss obstacles encountered during implementation and how they were resolved.
3. **Results and Impact:**
   - **Metrics:** Present quantitative data (e.g., performance improvements, cost savings) to demonstrate success.
   - **Qualitative Outcomes:** Share customer feedback or operational improvements.
   - **Scalability:** Discuss how the solution can be scaled or adapted to other contexts.
4. **Interactive Elements:**
   - **Simulations:** Include code examples or interactive dashboards that allow readers to experiment with parameters.
   - **Q&A Sections:** Pose reflective questions to guide the reader in applying the lessons learned to their own projects.

Real-World Case Study: Autonomous Customer Service Chatbot

117

Background:

A financial services firm needed to improve its customer service operations. Traditional call centers were overwhelmed, and response times were slow. The goal was to deploy an autonomous customer service chatbot that could handle routine inquiries, process transactions, and escalate complex issues to human operators.

Implementation Details:

- **Technology Stack:**
    - **Platform:** Deployed using TensorFlow for natural language processing (NLP) and reinforcement learning.
    - **Integration:** Connected to the company's CRM system for real-time data access.
    - **User Interface:** Available through both a mobile app and web interface.
- **Process Flow:**
    - **Data Collection:**
        - Customer inquiries were collected from chat logs and call center transcripts.
    - **Model Training:**
        - A neural network was trained to understand common queries and classify them into categories.
    - **Decision-Making:**
        - Reinforcement learning was used to optimize responses over time.
    - **Action and Feedback:**
        - The chatbot provided immediate responses and logged customer satisfaction scores for continuous improvement.
- **Challenges and Resolutions:**
    - **Ambiguity in Queries:**
      Addressed by incorporating context-aware NLP models.
    - **Integration Issues:**
      Solved by establishing a robust API framework that ensured smooth data flow between systems.

Results and Impact:

- **Metrics:**
    - 40% reduction in call center volume.
    - 30% improvement in average response time.
    - High customer satisfaction ratings.
- **Scalability:**
    - The solution was later expanded to handle multi-language support and additional service domains.

Interactive Element:

Below is a simplified simulation in Python that mimics a basic decision-making process of an autonomous chatbot. This code lets you experiment with response selection based on simulated customer input.

python

```python
import random


def simulate_customer_input():
    # Simulate a list of common customer inquiries
    inquiries = [
        "What is my account balance?",
        "How do I reset my password?",
        "I need help with a transaction.",
        "Tell me about your latest offers.",
        "I want to speak with a human agent."
    ]
    return random.choice(inquiries)


def classify_inquiry(inquiry):
    # A simple heuristic-based classification (in reality, use NLP models)
    if "balance" in inquiry:
        return "Account Inquiry"
    elif "password" in inquiry:
```

```python
        return "Password Reset"
    elif "transaction" in inquiry:
        return "Transaction Help"
    elif "offer" in inquiry:
        return "Promotional Inquiry"
    else:
        return "Escalate to Human"


def generate_response(category):
    responses = {
        "Account Inquiry": "Your current balance is $1,234.56.",
        "Password Reset": "Please follow the instructions sent to your email.",
        "Transaction Help": "I have forwarded your request to our transaction team.",
        "Promotional Inquiry": "Check out our latest offers on our website.",
        "Escalate to Human": "Please hold while I transfer you to a human agent."
    }
    return responses.get(category, "I'm sorry, I didn't understand your request.")


# Simulation loop
print("Autonomous Chatbot Simulation:")
for _ in range(5):
    inquiry = simulate_customer_input()
```

```python
print(f"\nCustomer Inquiry: {inquiry}")

category = classify_inquiry(inquiry)

print(f"Classified as: {category}")

response = generate_response(category)

print(f"Chatbot Response: {response}")
```

Explanation:

- **simulate_customer_input:**
  Randomly selects a customer inquiry from a predefined list.
- **classify_inquiry:**
  Uses simple keyword-based heuristics to classify the inquiry into categories.
- **generate_response:**
  Returns a predefined response based on the classification.
- **Simulation Loop:**
  Runs multiple iterations to simulate different customer inquiries and chatbot responses.

Summary

- **Startups and Disruptive Innovations:**
  We explored how agile startups leverage agentic AI to disrupt traditional industries by automating processes, optimizing operations, and delivering innovative, data-driven solutions. A table of hypothetical examples illustrates the variety of sectors impacted.
- **Real-World Success Stories and Case Studies:**
  Detailed case studies demonstrate how agentic AI is applied in real-world settings, with clear breakdowns of implementation, challenges, results, and interactive elements for hands-on learning.

These comprehensive insights help illustrate not only the theory but also the practical, transformative potential of agentic AI in both business and consumer domains, providing valuable lessons for innovators and practitioners alike.

Chapter 8 Leveraging Agentic AI in the Workplace

Agentic AI can revolutionize the workplace by automating routine tasks, streamlining operations, and transforming traditional workflows. By integrating intelligent systems into everyday business processes, organizations can boost productivity, reduce errors, and free up human resources for more strategic and creative tasks. This section explores how agentic AI enhances productivity through automation and transforms established workflows.

8.1. Enhancing Productivity Through Automation

Overview

Automation powered by agentic AI involves deploying systems that can independently perform routine, repetitive, or time-consuming tasks. By handling these tasks autonomously, AI frees employees to focus on higher-value activities such as decision-making, innovation, and customer engagement.

Key Areas of Productivity Enhancement

1. **Task Automation:**
   - **Data Entry and Processing:** AI systems can extract, validate, and process large volumes of data quickly and accurately.
   - **Scheduling and Calendar Management:** Automated scheduling tools optimize meeting times, adjust calendars based on priorities, and manage resource allocation.
   - **Email and Communication Management:** Intelligent assistants can sort emails, generate responses, and prioritize urgent messages.
2. **Process Optimization:**
   - **Automated Reporting:** AI generates regular performance reports and dashboards, reducing manual reporting time.
   - **Workflow Management:** AI systems monitor ongoing projects, flag bottlenecks, and suggest adjustments to improve throughput.
3. **Enhanced Decision-Making:**
   - **Real-Time Analytics:** Automated data analysis and visualization tools provide timely insights, enabling faster and better-informed decisions.
   - **Predictive Maintenance:** In operational settings, AI predicts equipment failures and schedules maintenance, reducing downtime.

Table: Examples of Productivity Automation

Task Area	Automated Function	Benefits
Data Processing	Automated data extraction, validation, and entry	Reduces human error; accelerates processing
Scheduling & Calendar Management	Intelligent scheduling based on priority and availability	Saves time; optimizes resource utilization
Communication Management	Email filtering and automated responses	Improves response time; reduces workload
Reporting	Automated generation of dashboards and performance reports	Enhances decision-making with timely insights
Maintenance & Operations	Predictive maintenance scheduling using sensor data	Minimizes downtime; extends equipment life

Example: Automated Email Sorting Agent

Below is a simplified Python code example illustrating an autonomous email sorting agent. This agent categorizes incoming emails based on keywords and directs them to appropriate folders.

python

```
import re
```

```python
# Sample emails represented as a list of dictionaries
emails = [

    {"subject": "Meeting Reminder", "body": "Don't forget our meeting at 10 AM.", "from": "boss@example.com"},

    {"subject": "Invoice Attached", "body": "Please find the attached invoice for last month.", "from": "accounts@example.com"},

    {"subject": "Social Event", "body": "Join us for a team lunch on Friday.", "from": "hr@example.com"}

]


# Define simple rules for categorization based on keywords in subject or body
def categorize_email(email):
    subject = email["subject"].lower()
    body = email["body"].lower()


    if re.search("invoice", subject) or re.search("invoice", body):
        return "Finance"
    elif re.search("meeting", subject) or re.search("meeting", body):
        return "Meetings"
    elif re.search("lunch", subject) or re.search("event", subject):
        return "Social"
    else:
        return "General"
```

```
# Process each email and print the categorized result

for email in emails:

    category = categorize_email(email)

    print(f"Email Subject: '{email['subject']}' categorized as: {category}")
```

Explanation:

- **Input:** A list of sample email messages.
- **Categorization:** The function categorize_email uses simple keyword matching to determine the category.
- **Output:** Emails are assigned to folders like "Finance," "Meetings," "Social," or "General," which automates part of the email management process.

8.2. Transforming Traditional Workflows with AI

Overview

Traditional workflows in many organizations are manual, siloed, and inflexible. Agentic AI transforms these workflows by introducing automation, real-time monitoring, and adaptive decision-making. This leads to more agile processes and better alignment with dynamic business needs.

Key Areas of Workflow Transformation

1. **Integration of Data Streams:**
   - **Unified Data Processing:** AI can merge data from various sources—sales, customer feedback, operational metrics—to provide a holistic view of performance.
   - **Real-Time Monitoring:** Continuous data analysis enables immediate detection of issues and opportunities.
2. **Process Reengineering:**
   - **Dynamic Routing:** Automated systems can reroute tasks or adjust resource allocation on the fly, based on real-time performance indicators.
   - **Adaptive Scheduling:** AI optimizes project timelines by anticipating delays and reallocating tasks dynamically.
3. **Enhanced Collaboration:**

- **Shared Dashboards and Reporting:** Interactive dashboards allow teams to monitor progress and collaborate on decision-making.
- **Workflow Automation Tools:** Platforms like robotic process automation (RPA) integrate with existing systems to streamline operations.
4. **Customer-Facing Transformations:**
    - **Personalized Experiences:** AI tailors workflows for customer support, marketing, and sales to meet individual needs.
    - **Self-Service Portals:** Intelligent agents provide customers with automated assistance, reducing the workload on support teams.

Table: Transforming Traditional Workflows with AI

Workflow Area	Traditional Approach	AI-Enhanced Approach	Benefits
Data Integration	Manual data consolidation from different departments	Unified, real-time data pipelines with automated analytics	Improved decision-making and efficiency
Task Routing	Static task assignments based on fixed schedules	Dynamic routing based on real-time workload and performance	Greater agility and responsiveness
Reporting	Periodic manual reports	Continuous, interactive dashboards	Timely insights and better collaboration
Customer Support	Relying on human agents for all queries	Automated chatbots and virtual assistants	Faster response times and reduced operational costs

Project Scheduling	Fixed schedules with little flexibility	Adaptive scheduling that adjusts to unforeseen delays	Enhanced productivity and timely project delivery

Example: Adaptive Task Routing Simulation

Below is a Python code example simulating an adaptive task routing system. The system assigns tasks to team members based on current workload and task priority.

python

```python
import random


# Sample data: team members with current workload (number of tasks)
team_members = {
    "Alice": 3,
    "Bob": 5,
    "Charlie": 2,
    "Dana": 4
}


# List of tasks with priorities (higher value indicates higher priority)
tasks = [
    {"task": "Prepare report", "priority": 3},
    {"task": "Client meeting", "priority": 5},
    {"task": "Update website", "priority": 2},
```

```python
    {"task": "Process invoices", "priority": 4}
]


def assign_task(members, task):
    """
    Assign a task to the team member with the lowest workload.
    Priority can influence assignment if needed.
    """
    # Identify the team member with the minimum workload
    selected_member = min(members, key=members.get)
    # Update workload: add one task
    members[selected_member] += 1
    return selected_member


# Simulate task assignment
print("Task Assignment Simulation:")
for task in tasks:
    assignee = assign_task(team_members, task)
    print(f"Task: '{task['task']}' (Priority: {task['priority']}) assigned to {assignee}")


print("\nUpdated Team Workloads:")
for member, workload in team_members.items():
    print(f"{member}: {workload} tasks")
```

Explanation:

- **Team Members:**
  A dictionary represents team members and their current workloads.
- **Tasks:**
  A list of tasks, each with a priority level.
- **Assignment Function:**
  The function assign_task assigns each new task to the team member with the lowest current workload.
- **Simulation:**
  The code iterates through tasks and assigns them, then prints updated workloads to demonstrate how AI can dynamically balance tasks.

Summary

- **Enhancing Productivity Through Automation:**
  Agentic AI automates routine tasks—such as data processing, scheduling, and communication management—leading to significant productivity gains. The email sorting and inventory management examples illustrate how automation reduces manual effort and improves efficiency.
- **Transforming Traditional Workflows with AI:**
  Traditional workflows are reengineered by integrating real-time data, dynamic task routing, and adaptive scheduling. The adaptive task routing simulation shows how AI can streamline operations and balance workloads, transforming the way teams collaborate and manage projects.

Together, these approaches highlight the potential of agentic AI to drive workplace efficiency and innovation, making it a critical tool for modern businesses and organizations.

8.3. Integrating Human Expertise with AI Systems

Overview

While agentic AI systems can process vast amounts of data and automate routine tasks, the best outcomes often result from combining these capabilities with human expertise. Human oversight, judgment, and domain knowledge can complement AI's data-driven insights. Together, they form a hybrid system that leverages the strengths of both—improving accuracy, fostering innovation, and ensuring ethical decision-making.

Key Areas of Integration

1. **Decision Augmentation:**
   - **AI-Driven Insights:** AI systems analyze data and suggest recommendations.
   - **Human Judgment:** Experts review these recommendations and consider contextual, ethical, or strategic factors that AI might miss.
2. **Error Checking and Quality Control:**
   - **Automated Monitoring:** AI continuously monitors processes and flags anomalies.
   - **Expert Review:** Human experts assess flagged issues to determine if intervention is necessary.
3. **Continuous Learning:**
   - **Feedback Loop:** Human experts provide feedback on AI decisions, which is then used to refine algorithms and improve performance over time.
4. **Customization and Adaptation:**
   - **Domain-Specific Knowledge:** Humans can tailor AI systems to industry-specific challenges by adjusting parameters, setting policies, and refining workflows.

Comparative Table: Roles in a Hybrid AI-Human System

Function	AI Contribution	Human Expertise Contribution
Data Analysis	Processes large volumes of data; identifies trends.	Interprets trends in context; adds qualitative insights.
Decision-Making	Provides recommendations based on statistical models.	Applies judgment; considers ethical and strategic factors.

Error Detection	Flags outliers and anomalies automatically.	Investigates and confirms errors; makes final decisions.
Process Optimization	Suggests process improvements based on data patterns.	Prioritizes improvements; integrates industry experience.
Continuous Improvement	Updates models based on feedback loops.	Provides corrective feedback; refines decision criteria.

Example: Hybrid Decision-Making Simulation

Below is a Python code example simulating a simple hybrid decision-making process. In this simulation, an AI model suggests an action based on data analysis, and then a human expert reviews and finalizes the decision. This process is common in scenarios such as financial investment, healthcare diagnostics, or customer service.

python

```
import random


def ai_recommendation(data):
    """

    AI component: Generate a recommendation based on input data.

    Here, we simulate a simple recommendation based on whether the data
value is above or below a threshold.

    """

    threshold = 50
```

```python
    if data > threshold:

        return "Action A"  # Example: Invest, approve treatment, etc.

    else:

        return "Action B"  # Example: Divest, further test, etc.


def human_expertise(review_data, ai_decision):

    """

    Human component: Review the AI recommendation along with
    additional context or experience.

    The expert can override the AI decision based on contextual factors.

    """

    # Simulate a decision factor from human expertise (e.g., risk assessment,
    ethical considerations)

    risk_factor = random.uniform(0, 1)

    # If risk factor is high, prefer the alternative decision

    if risk_factor > 0.7:

        final_decision = "Action B" if ai_decision == "Action A" else "Action A"

    else:

        final_decision = ai_decision

    return final_decision, risk_factor


# Simulation of hybrid decision-making

data_sample = random.randint(30, 70)  # Simulated input data

print(f"Input Data: {data_sample}")
```

```python
# AI makes an initial recommendation
ai_decision = ai_recommendation(data_sample)
print(f"AI Recommendation: {ai_decision}")


# Human expert reviews the decision
final_decision, risk_factor = human_expertise(data_sample, ai_decision)
print(f"Human Risk Factor: {risk_factor:.2f}")
print(f"Final Decision after Human Review: {final_decision}")
```

Explanation:

- **AI Component:**
  The ai_recommendation function simulates an AI model that makes a recommendation (e.g., "Action A" or "Action B") based on a threshold.
- **Human Component:**
  The human_expertise function simulates a human expert reviewing the AI's recommendation. A randomly generated risk factor influences whether the expert agrees or overrides the AI's suggestion.
- **Hybrid Decision:**
  The simulation prints both the AI's initial recommendation and the final decision after human review, demonstrating how human expertise can be integrated into the decision-making loop.

Benefits of Integrating Human Expertise

- **Improved Accuracy:**
  Combining quantitative data analysis with qualitative judgment leads to more accurate and reliable outcomes.
- **Ethical Considerations:**
  Human oversight helps ensure that decisions align with ethical and social values.
- **Adaptive Learning:**
  Feedback from human experts allows AI models to continuously improve and adapt to new contexts.

- **Risk Management:**
  Human judgment provides an additional layer of risk assessment, critical in high-stakes environments.

8.4. Case Studies: Marketing, Operations, and Beyond

Overview

Case studies provide concrete examples of how agentic AI is transforming various aspects of the workplace. In this section, we review real-world examples and interactive case studies from marketing, operations, and other domains. These examples illustrate both the benefits and challenges of integrating AI into existing workflows.

Case Study Components

1. **Background and Objectives:**
   - **Context:** Describe the business environment or industry.
   - **Goal:** Outline the problem the organization aimed to solve with agentic AI.
2. **Implementation Details:**
   - **Technology Stack:** Explain the AI models, tools, and platforms used.
   - **Workflow Integration:** Describe how the AI system was integrated into the existing workflow.
   - **Challenges:** Discuss any difficulties encountered during implementation and the solutions adopted.
3. **Results and Impact:**
   - **Quantitative Metrics:** Provide data on improvements (e.g., increased sales, reduced processing time).
   - **Qualitative Outcomes:** Include testimonials or feedback from users.
   - **Scalability:** Explain how the solution can be expanded or adapted to other areas.
4. **Interactive Elements:**
   - **Simulations:** Offer code examples or dashboards that allow users to explore parameters.
   - **Discussion Questions:** Include questions to prompt reflection on how similar solutions could be applied in other contexts.

Example 1: Marketing Automation in Retail

Background:
A retail company sought to improve its digital marketing efforts by leveraging agentic AI to personalize customer engagement and optimize ad spend.

Implementation:

- **Technology Stack:**
  - AI algorithms for customer segmentation and behavior analysis.
  - Integration with CRM and digital advertising platforms.
- **Workflow Integration:**
  - Automated data collection from social media, website interactions, and sales data.
  - Real-time analytics used to adjust marketing strategies dynamically.
- **Challenges:**
  - Data integration from multiple sources.
  - Ensuring real-time responsiveness without compromising data quality.

Results:

- **Metrics:**
  - 25% increase in customer engagement.
  - 20% reduction in advertising costs due to optimized targeting.
- **Feedback:**
  - Marketers reported improved efficiency and deeper customer insights.
- **Scalability:**
  - The solution was adapted to additional product lines and expanded to other regions.

Example 2: Operations Optimization in Manufacturing

Background:
A manufacturing firm implemented agentic AI to streamline production processes, reduce downtime, and enhance quality control.

Implementation:

- **Technology Stack:**
  - AI-powered predictive maintenance models.
  - Integration with IoT sensors and production line control systems.
- **Workflow Integration:**
  - Continuous monitoring of machine performance.

- ○ Automated alerts and scheduling for preventive maintenance.
- **Challenges:**
  - ○ Managing sensor data volume and variability.
  - ○ Integrating AI recommendations with existing maintenance schedules.

Results:

- **Metrics:**
  - ○ 30% reduction in unplanned downtime.
  - ○ 15% increase in overall production efficiency.
- **Feedback:**
  - ○ Operations teams appreciated the proactive approach and cost savings.
- **Scalability:**
  - ○ The system was later deployed across multiple plants.

Interactive Case Study: Exploring Marketing Optimization

Below is a simplified Python code example that simulates a marketing optimization scenario. This simulation allows you to experiment with customer segmentation and ad targeting based on random customer data.

python

```python
import numpy as np

import pandas as pd

import matplotlib.pyplot as plt

import seaborn as sns


# Simulate customer data

np.random.seed(42)

customer_data = pd.DataFrame({

    "CustomerID": range(1, 101),

    "Age": np.random.randint(18, 65, size=100),
```

```
    "AnnualIncome": np.random.randint(30000, 120000, size=100),

    "SpendingScore": np.random.randint(1, 100, size=100)  # Higher score
indicates more spending

})



# Simple segmentation: group customers into two segments based on
Spending Score

customer_data['Segment'] = np.where(customer_data['SpendingScore'] >
50, 'High-Value', 'Low-Value')



# Display segmentation results

print(customer_data.head())



# Visualize the segmentation

plt.figure(figsize=(10, 6))

sns.scatterplot(data=customer_data, x="AnnualIncome",
y="SpendingScore", hue="Segment", palette="Set1")

plt.title("Customer Segmentation Based on Annual Income and Spending
Score")

plt.xlabel("Annual Income ($)")

plt.ylabel("Spending Score")

plt.show()
```

Explanation:

- **Data Simulation:**
Customer data is generated with random values for age, income, and spending score.
- **Segmentation:**
Customers are segmented into "High-Value" and "Low-Value" based on a spending score threshold.
- **Visualization:**
A scatter plot visualizes how the segments distribute over income and spending, providing insights into targeted marketing strategies.
- **Interactive Element:**
Users can modify segmentation thresholds or explore different variables to see how customer segments change.

Summary

- **Integrating Human Expertise with AI Systems:**
A hybrid approach that combines the analytical power of AI with human judgment leads to more effective and ethical decision-making. Tables and code examples illustrate how AI recommendations can be reviewed and refined by human experts.
- **Case Studies: Marketing, Operations, and Beyond:**
Real-world examples demonstrate the transformative impact of agentic AI across industries. Detailed case studies in retail marketing and manufacturing operations highlight implementation details, challenges, and measurable outcomes, while interactive simulations allow users to explore practical applications.

8.5. Quick Reference Guides and Checklists

Overview

In dynamic workplace environments where agentic AI systems are deployed, quick reference guides and checklists serve as invaluable tools. They provide concise, actionable information that helps teams efficiently execute tasks, troubleshoot issues, and maintain best practices. These resources reduce cognitive load, ensure consistency, and serve as a ready reference for both new team members and experienced practitioners.

Importance of Quick Reference Guides and Checklists

1. **Efficiency and Consistency:**
Quick reference guides distill complex processes into clear, step-by-step

instructions, ensuring that critical tasks are performed consistently every time. This is particularly important in AI-driven environments where even minor deviations can lead to errors or performance issues.

2. **Onboarding and Training:**
New team members benefit from concise checklists that highlight essential steps and best practices. They provide a roadmap to quickly become productive while reducing the learning curve associated with complex systems.

3. **Error Reduction and Troubleshooting:**
Checklists act as a safeguard by ensuring that all necessary steps are followed, reducing the likelihood of oversights. In troubleshooting scenarios, reference guides help quickly identify potential issues and suggest remedial actions.

4. **Rapid Decision Making:**
In fast-paced operations, having immediate access to critical information speeds up decision-making processes. Quick guides help teams respond promptly to changes, whether it's adjusting AI model parameters or handling an unexpected system alert.

Components of a Quick Reference Guide

A well-designed quick reference guide or checklist for agentic AI systems typically includes the following elements:

- **Task Description:**
A brief explanation of the task or process, outlining its purpose and importance.

- **Step-by-Step Instructions:**
A clear, sequential list of actions required to complete the task. Each step should be concise and actionable.

- **Key Parameters and Thresholds:**
Important values (e.g., error margins, performance indicators) that need to be monitored or adjusted.

- **Troubleshooting Tips:**
Common issues that may arise during the process and recommended corrective measures.

- **Reference Links or Resources:**
Pointers to more detailed documentation or related materials for further reading.

Example Table: Quick Reference Guide for Agentic AI Deployment

Section	Description/Steps	Key Points/Thresholds

System Check	Verify that all sensors and communication interfaces are operational.	All sensors reporting within normal range.
Data Collection	Ensure data streams are active and data is being logged correctly.	Check data frequency and integrity.
Model Initialization	Load pre-trained models and verify that hyperparameters match deployment settings.	Confirm learning rate, batch size, etc.
Decision Loop Activation	Start the decision loop and monitor initial outputs.	Monitor initial errors; adjust thresholds if needed.
Error Handling	Follow the troubleshooting steps if errors exceed predefined thresholds.	Error threshold: ±0.1 for sensor inputs.
System Shutdown/Restart	Follow the proper protocol to safely shut down or restart the system in case of a critical fault.	Backup logs before shutdown.

Example: Simple Checklist in Python

To illustrate how a digital checklist might be implemented, here's a sample Python script that simulates a checklist for a basic AI system startup. This script prompts the user to confirm each step, ensuring that all key actions are completed before deployment.

python

```python
def checklist():
    steps = [
        "Verify sensor functionality.",
        "Confirm data streams are active.",
        "Load pre-trained models.",
        "Check model hyperparameters (e.g., learning rate, batch size).",
        "Activate decision loop and monitor initial outputs.",
        "Review error thresholds and system logs.",
        "Initiate system startup sequence."
    ]

    print("=== Agentic AI System Startup Checklist ===\n")
    for index, step in enumerate(steps, start=1):
        input(f"Step {index}: {step} [Press Enter to confirm]")
        print(f"Step {index} confirmed.\n")

    print("All checklist items confirmed. System startup complete.")

if __name__ == "__main__":
    checklist()
```

Explanation:

- **Checklist Function:**
  The checklist function contains a list of sequential steps required for starting up an agentic AI system.
- **User Prompts:**
  Each step is presented to the user, who must press Enter to confirm that the step has been completed. This mimics a physical checklist where items are ticked off.
- **Confirmation:**
  After all steps are confirmed, the script outputs a message indicating that the system startup is complete.

Best Practices for Creating Quick Reference Guides

- **Clarity and Conciseness:**
  Ensure that instructions are written in simple language and are free from ambiguity.
- **Visual Aids:**
  Where possible, include flowcharts, diagrams, or screenshots to support the text.
- **Regular Updates:**
  Keep the guides up-to-date with the latest system configurations and best practices.
- **Accessibility:**
  Make guides easily accessible in both digital and print formats so that they can be quickly referenced in any setting.

Summary

Quick reference guides and checklists are essential tools for leveraging agentic AI in the workplace. They streamline complex processes into manageable steps, aid in onboarding and troubleshooting, and promote consistency and efficiency. By creating well-structured, easily accessible guides, organizations can enhance productivity, reduce errors, and empower both AI systems and human teams to work in harmony.

Chapter 9 Ethics, Privacy, and Governance

As agentic AI systems become more integrated into society, addressing ethical considerations, privacy, and governance becomes essential. These systems influence decisions that can have significant societal impacts, making it crucial to ensure that they operate fairly, transparently, and responsibly.

9.1. Ethical Considerations for Autonomous Systems

Overview

Ethical considerations for autonomous systems focus on the responsible development, deployment, and management of AI. This involves ensuring that AI systems are designed to respect human rights, uphold societal values, and minimize unintended harm.

Key Ethical Areas

1. **Accountability and Transparency:**
   - **Explanation:**
     Autonomous systems must provide clear explanations for their decisions. Transparency ensures that stakeholders understand how and why a system arrived at a particular outcome.
   - **Implementation:**
     Use explainable AI (XAI) techniques that generate human-interpretable explanations alongside model predictions.
2. **Safety and Reliability:**
   - **Explanation:**
     Safety measures must be in place to prevent harmful actions, especially when autonomous systems operate in critical environments such as healthcare or transportation.
   - **Implementation:**
     Incorporate rigorous testing, continuous monitoring, and fail-safe mechanisms.
3. **Consent and Privacy:**
   - **Explanation:**
     AI systems must respect individual privacy and obtain consent before using personal data. This includes ensuring that data collection and processing are compliant with legal regulations.

- ○ **Implementation:**
  Adopt data anonymization techniques, secure data storage, and clear consent protocols.
4. **Impact on Employment and Society:**
   - ○ **Explanation:**
     Consideration must be given to the socio-economic impact of automation, particularly regarding job displacement and social inequality.
   - ○ **Implementation:**
     Develop strategies for workforce reskilling and ensure that AI benefits are widely distributed.

Table: Ethical Considerations for Autonomous Systems

Ethical Aspect	Description	Examples/Actions
Accountability	Clear assignment of responsibility for AI decisions.	Maintain audit trails, use XAI techniques.
Transparency	Providing understandable insights into decision-making processes.	Publish model details and decision criteria.
Safety	Ensuring the system operates without causing harm.	Implement redundancy, emergency shut-offs, and rigorous testing.
Privacy and Consent	Protecting personal data and obtaining user consent.	Use encryption, anonymization, and adhere to GDPR/CCPA.

| Societal Impact | Balancing technological advances with human welfare. | Promote workforce training and consider ethical implications of automation. |

Practical Example: Explainable AI for Ethical Transparency

Below is a simplified Python example using the LIME (Local Interpretable Model-agnostic Explanations) library to explain predictions from a machine learning model. This approach can enhance transparency by providing human-interpretable explanations for individual predictions.

python

```python
import numpy as np

import pandas as pd

from sklearn.datasets import load_iris

from sklearn.model_selection import train_test_split

from sklearn.ensemble import RandomForestClassifier

import lime

import lime.lime_tabular


# Load and prepare the Iris dataset

iris = load_iris()

X = iris.data

y = iris.target

feature_names = iris.feature_names

class_names = iris.target_names
```

```python
X_train, X_test, y_train, y_test = train_test_split(X, y, test_size=0.2,
random_state=42)


# Train a RandomForestClassifier

clf = RandomForestClassifier(n_estimators=100, random_state=42)

clf.fit(X_train, y_train)


# Initialize LIME explainer for tabular data

explainer = lime.lime_tabular.LimeTabularExplainer(

    training_data=X_train,

    feature_names=feature_names,

    class_names=class_names,

    mode='classification'

)


# Explain a single prediction

i = 1  # Index of a test instance

exp = explainer.explain_instance(X_test[i], clf.predict_proba,
num_features=4)

exp.show_in_notebook(show_all=False)
```

Explanation:

- **Data Preparation:**
  The Iris dataset is loaded, split, and used to train a RandomForestClassifier.

146

- **LIME Explainer:**
  The LimeTabularExplainer is set up using the training data, feature names, and class names.
- **Explanation Generation:**
  An explanation for a single test instance is generated, which highlights the most influential features affecting the prediction.
- **Outcome:**
  This process helps end users understand why the model made a specific prediction, fostering transparency and ethical accountability.

9.2. Addressing Bias and Ensuring Fairness

Overview

Bias in AI can lead to unfair treatment of individuals or groups, reinforcing existing inequalities. Ensuring fairness involves proactively identifying, mitigating, and monitoring biases throughout the AI lifecycle.

Sources of Bias

1. **Data Bias:**
   - **Explanation:**
     Data used to train AI models may reflect historical prejudices or imbalances.
   - **Mitigation:**
     Use diverse and representative datasets; perform bias audits on training data.
2. **Algorithmic Bias:**
   - **Explanation:**
     Certain algorithms might amplify biases present in the data.
   - **Mitigation:**
     Apply fairness-aware algorithms and techniques that adjust for bias during model training.
3. **Human Bias:**
   - **Explanation:**
     Bias can be introduced by human decisions during data labeling, model selection, or interpretation.
   - **Mitigation:**
     Incorporate multiple perspectives, use blind evaluation processes, and involve domain experts in critical decisions.

Ensuring Fairness

- **Fairness Metrics:**
  Define and measure fairness using metrics such as disparate impact, equal opportunity, or demographic parity.
- **Bias Auditing:**
  Regularly audit AI models to identify and rectify biases. This can be automated with tools that assess model outputs across different demographic groups.
- **Regulatory Compliance:**
  Ensure AI systems adhere to legal frameworks and guidelines such as GDPR in Europe or the Equal Credit Opportunity Act in the U.S.

Table: Strategies for Bias Mitigation and Fairness

Bias Source	Mitigation Strategy	Example/Action
Data Bias	Use diverse, balanced datasets; data augmentation; bias audits.	Augment underrepresented classes in training data.
Algorithmic Bias	Implement fairness-aware algorithms; adjust loss functions to penalize biased outcomes.	Use algorithms that enforce equal opportunity across groups.
Human Bias	Standardize data labeling; use blind evaluation; involve multiple reviewers.	Implement double-blind reviews in data annotation processes.

Practical Example: Evaluating Fairness in a Classification Model

Below is a Python example that demonstrates how to evaluate fairness using the concept of disparate impact. In this example, we simulate evaluating a classifier on a sensitive attribute.

python

```python
import numpy as np

import pandas as pd

from sklearn.metrics import accuracy_score


# Simulated data for demonstration

data = {

    'feature': np.random.rand(100),

    'sensitive_attribute': np.random.choice(['Group A', 'Group B'], 100),

    'label': np.random.choice([0, 1], 100)

}

df = pd.DataFrame(data)


# Simulate predictions from a classifier

df['prediction'] = np.random.choice([0, 1], 100)


# Calculate accuracy for each group

accuracy_group_a = accuracy_score(df[df['sensitive_attribute'] == 'Group A']['label'],

                    df[df['sensitive_attribute'] == 'Group A']['prediction'])

accuracy_group_b = accuracy_score(df[df['sensitive_attribute'] == 'Group B']['label'],

                    df[df['sensitive_attribute'] == 'Group B']['prediction'])
```

```python
print("Accuracy for Group A: {:.2f}".format(accuracy_group_a))

print("Accuracy for Group B: {:.2f}".format(accuracy_group_b))


# Calculate disparate impact as the ratio of accuracy between groups

disparate_impact = accuracy_group_a / accuracy_group_b if
accuracy_group_b != 0 else np.inf

print("Disparate Impact Ratio (Group A / Group B):
{:.2f}".format(disparate_impact))
```

Explanation:

- **Data Simulation:**
  A dataset is created with a continuous feature, a sensitive attribute (two groups), and binary labels.
- **Predictions:**
  Random predictions simulate the output of a classifier.
- **Group Accuracy Calculation:**
  The code calculates accuracy separately for each sensitive group.
- **Disparate Impact Ratio:**
  The ratio of the accuracy of one group over the other is computed as a measure of fairness. A ratio close to 1 indicates fairness; significant deviations may signal bias.

Summary

- **Ethical Considerations for Autonomous Systems:**
  Emphasize accountability, transparency, safety, privacy, and the broader societal impact. Implementing explainable AI techniques and rigorous testing enhances ethical standards.
- **Addressing Bias and Ensuring Fairness:**
  Mitigate data, algorithmic, and human biases by employing diverse datasets, fairness-aware algorithms, and standardized evaluation processes. Regular bias audits and adherence to fairness metrics help maintain equity in AI systems.

By incorporating these ethical guidelines and fairness strategies into the development and deployment of agentic AI, organizations can build systems that not only perform effectively but also respect individual rights and promote societal well-being.

9.3. Privacy, Security, and Data Protection

Overview

Privacy, security, and data protection are critical concerns in the development and deployment of agentic AI systems. Since these systems rely heavily on large volumes of data—often including sensitive or personal information—ensuring that data is securely managed and that user privacy is preserved is paramount. This section covers the best practices, strategies, and technical measures necessary to safeguard data throughout its lifecycle.

Key Concepts

1. **Privacy:**
   - **Definition:**
     The right of individuals to control how their personal data is collected, used, and shared. Privacy in AI involves ensuring that data is processed in a manner that respects individual consent and confidentiality.
   - **Best Practices:**
     - Implement clear data usage policies.
     - Obtain explicit consent from users before collecting personal data.
     - Anonymize or pseudonymize data to protect individual identities.
2. **Security:**
   - **Definition:**
     The protection of data from unauthorized access, breaches, or attacks. In the context of agentic AI, security measures ensure that both the data and the AI system itself are resilient against cyber threats.
   - **Best Practices:**
     - Use encryption to secure data at rest and in transit.
     - Implement robust access controls and authentication mechanisms.
     - Regularly update and patch systems to protect against vulnerabilities.
3. **Data Protection:**
   - **Definition:**
     Policies and technologies designed to safeguard data integrity, confidentiality, and availability. Data protection encompasses the entire data lifecycle—from collection and storage to processing and deletion.

- ○ **Best Practices:**
  - Use secure storage solutions and backup systems.
  - Monitor data access and usage through audit logs.
  - Establish data retention policies to ensure data is not kept longer than necessary.

Table: Privacy, Security, and Data Protection Measures

Aspect	Description	Key Actions
Privacy	Protecting individual rights regarding personal data.	Implement consent mechanisms; anonymize data; transparent policies.
Security	Safeguarding data against unauthorized access and cyber threats.	Use encryption (AES, TLS); enforce multi-factor authentication; regular patching.
Data Protection	Maintaining data integrity and availability throughout its lifecycle.	Secure storage solutions; backup and disaster recovery; data retention policies.

Practical Example: Encrypting Data with Python

Below is a Python code example that demonstrates how to encrypt and decrypt sensitive data using the cryptographylibrary. This is one way to ensure that data remains secure during storage or transmission.

python

```python
from cryptography.fernet import Fernet
```

```python
# Step 1: Generate a key and instantiate a Fernet instance

key = Fernet.generate_key()

cipher_suite = Fernet(key)


# Display the key (in practice, store this securely)

print(f"Encryption Key: {key.decode()}")


# Step 2: Define the sensitive data to be encrypted

sensitive_data = "User's confidential data, e.g., personal identification information."

print(f"Original Data: {sensitive_data}")


# Step 3: Encrypt the data

encrypted_data = cipher_suite.encrypt(sensitive_data.encode())

print(f"Encrypted Data: {encrypted_data.decode()}")


# Step 4: Decrypt the data

decrypted_data = cipher_suite.decrypt(encrypted_data)

print(f"Decrypted Data: {decrypted_data.decode()}")
```

Explanation:

- **Key Generation:**
  A key is generated using Fernet.generate_key(), which is used for both encryption and decryption.

- **Encryption:**
  The sensitive data is encoded to bytes and then encrypted. The result is a secure, encoded string.
- **Decryption:**
  The encrypted data is decrypted back to the original string, ensuring data confidentiality and integrity.

Summary

Privacy, security, and data protection are interdependent facets that ensure that agentic AI systems are trustworthy and resilient. Implementing strong privacy policies, robust security measures, and comprehensive data protection practices is essential to safeguard sensitive information and maintain public trust in AI technologies.

9.4. Regulatory Landscape and Governance Models

Overview

The regulatory landscape and governance models provide the framework within which agentic AI systems must operate. Governments, industry bodies, and international organizations have established rules and guidelines to ensure that AI technologies are developed and deployed responsibly. This section examines the key regulations, compliance requirements, and governance structures that guide the ethical and legal use of AI.

Key Regulatory Frameworks

1. **General Data Protection Regulation (GDPR):**
   - **Region:** European Union
   - **Focus:** Data privacy and protection.
   - **Key Requirements:**
     - Explicit consent for data collection.
     - Right to access, rectify, and delete personal data.
     - Data minimization and purpose limitation.
2. **California Consumer Privacy Act (CCPA):**
   - **Region:** California, USA
   - **Focus:** Consumer rights regarding personal data.
   - **Key Requirements:**
     - Disclosure of data collection practices.
     - Consumer rights to opt out of data sales.

- Enhanced data protection measures.
3. **Industry-Specific Regulations:**
   o **Examples:**
     - HIPAA (Health Insurance Portability and Accountability Act) for healthcare data.
     - PCI-DSS (Payment Card Industry Data Security Standard) for financial transactions.
   o **Focus:** Protecting sensitive information specific to industries such as healthcare and finance.

Governance Models

Governance models for AI encompass the policies, procedures, and organizational structures that oversee AI development and deployment. Key aspects include:

1. **Internal Governance:**
   o **Definition:**
     Organizations establish internal policies and ethics boards to oversee AI projects.
   o **Components:**
     - Ethical guidelines and best practices.
     - Regular audits and impact assessments.
     - Cross-functional teams including legal, technical, and domain experts.
2. **External Governance:**
   o **Definition:**
     External bodies, such as regulatory agencies and industry consortia, provide oversight and enforce compliance with standards.
   o **Components:**
     - Certification programs for AI systems.
     - Industry-wide standards (e.g., ISO standards for AI).
     - Public reporting and transparency requirements.

Table: Overview of Key Regulations and Governance Models

Regulation/Governance	Region/Scope	Key Focus	Notable Requirements/Components

GDPR	European Union	Data privacy and protection	Consent, data minimization, right to erasure
CCPA	California, USA	Consumer rights regarding personal data	Transparency, opt-out rights, data security
HIPAA	USA (Healthcare)	Protection of patient health information	Secure storage, access controls, audit trails
PCI-DSS	Global (Financial)	Security standards for payment processing	Data encryption, secure network protocols, regular audits
Internal Governance Structures	Organizational	Ethical oversight and risk management	Ethics boards, internal audits, cross-functional teams
External Governance Bodies	Regulatory Agencies/Industry	Enforcement of standards and certification	Certification programs, public transparency, compliance audits

Best Practices for Compliance

- **Regular Audits:**
  Conduct internal and external audits to ensure compliance with applicable regulations.

- **Training and Awareness:**
  Educate staff about regulatory requirements and ethical practices in AI development.
- **Documentation and Reporting:**
  Maintain thorough documentation of data practices, decision-making processes, and model performance to demonstrate compliance.
- **Stakeholder Engagement:**
  Engage with regulators, industry bodies, and the public to stay updated on evolving standards and expectations.

Summary

- **Regulatory Landscape:**
  Agentic AI systems must adhere to strict data protection and privacy laws such as GDPR, CCPA, and industry-specific regulations. These regulations are designed to protect individual rights and ensure that AI systems are deployed responsibly.
- **Governance Models:**
  Both internal and external governance structures play crucial roles in overseeing AI practices. Organizations must implement robust internal policies and work with external bodies to meet compliance standards and maintain public trust.

By understanding and adhering to these regulatory frameworks and governance models, organizations can not only mitigate legal and ethical risks but also promote responsible AI development that benefits society as a whole.

9.5. Discussion: Balancing Innovation and Responsibility

As agentic AI continues to advance, organizations and policymakers face the challenge of balancing the drive for innovation with the need for responsibility. This balancing act is crucial not only for fostering technological progress but also for ensuring that AI systems are developed and deployed in ways that protect individuals, promote fairness, and benefit society as a whole. Below, we explore the key considerations, challenges, and strategies for achieving this balance.

Key Considerations

1. **Innovation Drivers:**
   - **Technological Advancements:**
     Rapid developments in computational power, data availability, and machine learning algorithms have accelerated AI innovation. This has led

to breakthroughs in areas like autonomous systems, natural language processing, and computer vision.

- **Economic Benefits:**
  AI-driven innovation promises significant gains in efficiency, cost reduction, and new business opportunities across various sectors such as healthcare, finance, manufacturing, and consumer services.
- **Competitive Advantage:**
  For businesses, adopting cutting-edge AI technologies can lead to a substantial competitive edge, enabling quicker decision-making, improved customer experiences, and operational excellence.

2. **Responsibility Imperatives:**
   - **Ethical Principles:**
     Responsible innovation in AI demands adherence to ethical principles such as transparency, accountability, fairness, and respect for privacy. These principles ensure that technological advancements do not come at the cost of societal well-being.
   - **Risk Management:**
     Balancing innovation with responsibility requires identifying and mitigating risks, including biases in data, potential harm from autonomous decision-making, and unintended social consequences.
   - **Regulatory Compliance:**
     Companies must navigate a complex landscape of regulations and standards (e.g., GDPR, CCPA, industry-specific guidelines) that aim to protect individual rights and ensure the safe deployment of AI technologies.

Challenges in Balancing Innovation and Responsibility

1. **Speed vs. Scrutiny:**
   - **Innovation Pace:**
     The rapid pace of AI development can pressure organizations to push new technologies to market quickly, sometimes at the expense of thorough ethical evaluation.
   - **Rigorous Oversight:**
     Implementing robust oversight and ethical review processes can slow down development but is essential for preventing harm and maintaining public trust.
2. **Complexity of AI Systems:**
   - **Black-Box Models:**
     Many advanced AI models, such as deep neural networks, operate as "black boxes" where the decision-making process is not easily

interpretable. This opacity makes it challenging to ensure transparency and accountability.

- ○ **Interdisciplinary Challenges:**
  Balancing innovation and responsibility requires collaboration among technical experts, ethicists, legal professionals, and industry stakeholders—a coordination effort that can be complex and resource-intensive.

3. **Economic and Social Trade-Offs:**
   - ○ **Disruptive Impact:**
     While AI innovation can lead to economic growth, it may also disrupt labor markets and exacerbate social inequalities. Responsible innovation must address these trade-offs by fostering inclusive growth and reskilling initiatives.
   - ○ **Global Variability:**
     Different regions have varying regulatory standards and cultural attitudes toward privacy and ethics, complicating the development of universally acceptable AI practices.

Strategies for Balancing Innovation and Responsibility

1. **Ethical Frameworks and Guidelines:**
   - ○ **Adopt and Adapt Standards:**
     Organizations can implement internationally recognized ethical frameworks, such as the IEEE Ethically Aligned Design or the European Commission's guidelines on trustworthy AI. These frameworks provide clear principles and best practices to guide development.
   - ○ **Develop Internal Ethics Boards:**
     Establishing multidisciplinary ethics committees within organizations can ensure continuous oversight and integration of ethical considerations throughout the AI lifecycle.

2. **Transparent and Explainable AI:**
   - ○ **Invest in Explainability:**
     Focusing on developing explainable AI models helps demystify decision-making processes, making it easier for stakeholders to understand and trust the technology.
   - ○ **Open Reporting:**
     Publishing transparent reports on model performance, including potential biases and limitations, encourages accountability and public trust.

3. **Iterative and Inclusive Development:**
   - ○ **Pilot Programs and Feedback Loops:**
     Implement pilot projects that allow for iterative testing and refinement.

Gathering feedback from diverse stakeholders—including users, impacted communities, and regulators—ensures that the technology addresses real-world needs and concerns.

- ○ **Collaboration and Partnerships:**
  Engaging with academic institutions, industry consortia, and civil society organizations can help share the burden of oversight and bring multiple perspectives to bear on complex ethical issues.

4. **Regulatory Engagement and Compliance:**
   - ○ **Proactive Regulation:**
     Companies should engage with regulators and participate in the development of new policies that balance innovation with societal needs.
   - ○ **Compliance and Best Practices:**
     Implement robust compliance measures and continuous monitoring systems to adhere to evolving legal and ethical standards.

Comparative Table: Innovation vs. Responsibility

Dimension	Innovation Focus	Responsibility Focus
Speed	Rapid development and market entry	Thorough ethical review and rigorous oversight
Transparency	Use of complex, high-performing "black-box" models	Emphasis on explainability and open reporting
Risk	Emphasis on competitive advantage and disruption	Focus on risk mitigation, fairness, and societal well-being
Economic Impact	Maximizing efficiency and cost reduction	Ensuring inclusive growth and mitigating adverse social effects

| **Regulatory Approach** | Minimal restrictions to foster experimentation | Comprehensive regulatory frameworks to protect individual rights |

Balancing innovation and responsibility is not a zero-sum game; rather, it is a dynamic process that requires constant vigilance, adaptability, and collaboration. By integrating ethical frameworks, investing in transparent AI, adopting iterative development practices, and engaging with regulatory bodies, organizations can harness the transformative power of agentic AI while ensuring that its benefits are realized in a manner that is safe, fair, and aligned with societal values.

This balanced approach is essential for fostering sustainable innovation that not only drives economic and technological progress but also upholds the ethical standards and public trust necessary for long-term success.

Chapter 10 Agentic AI in Decision Making and Strategy

Agentic AI is increasingly becoming an integral part of modern business strategy, enabling organizations to make faster, data-driven decisions. By automating routine analysis and offering autonomous insights, these systems help businesses anticipate market shifts, optimize operations, and craft strategies that are both agile and competitive. In this section, we examine the role of AI in business strategy and how autonomous insights enhance decision-making.

10.1. The Role of AI in Business Strategy

Overview

In today's rapidly evolving market, businesses must adapt quickly to remain competitive. AI plays a critical role by processing large volumes of data, identifying trends, and providing strategic recommendations that inform long-term planning. By integrating AI into business strategy, companies can optimize their operations, reduce costs, and discover new opportunities.

Key Areas Where AI Impacts Business Strategy:

1. **Market Analysis and Trend Forecasting:**
   - **Function:** AI analyzes market data—such as sales figures, customer behavior, and competitor activities—to identify emerging trends.
   - **Impact:** Enables proactive strategy adjustments, such as entering new markets or innovating product lines before competitors.
2. **Operational Efficiency:**
   - **Function:** By automating data analysis and monitoring operational metrics, AI identifies inefficiencies and recommends improvements.
   - **Impact:** Optimizes resource allocation, reduces waste, and streamlines processes.
3. **Customer Insights and Personalization:**
   - **Function:** AI-driven analytics segment customers based on behavior and preferences, enabling personalized marketing and service strategies.
   - **Impact:** Improves customer retention and boosts sales by tailoring offerings to individual needs.
4. **Risk Management:**

- ○ **Function:** AI models can predict potential risks by analyzing historical data and identifying patterns that precede adverse events.
- ○ **Impact:** Helps companies mitigate risks, safeguard investments, and maintain business continuity.

Table: AI's Strategic Impact on Business

Strategic Area	AI Function	Business Impact
Market Analysis	Trend forecasting using big data analytics	Proactive market positioning and competitive advantage.
Operational Efficiency	Process automation and resource optimization	Reduced costs, increased productivity, and streamlined operations.
Customer Personalization	Data-driven segmentation and predictive analytics	Enhanced customer satisfaction and loyalty.
Risk Management	Predictive risk modeling and anomaly detection	Better preparedness and reduced financial losses.

Example: Market Trend Analysis with Python

The following Python code demonstrates a simplified market trend analysis using a time series dataset. The code uses the pandas and matplotlib libraries to process sales data and visualize trends, a critical component in strategic decision-making.

python

```python
import pandas as pd

import matplotlib.pyplot as plt
```

```python
import numpy as np

# Simulate a time series dataset of monthly sales for two years
date_range = pd.date_range(start="2023-01-01", periods=24, freq="M")

sales = np.random.randint(100, 200, size=len(date_range))  # Random
sales data for demonstration


# Create a DataFrame
df = pd.DataFrame({

    "Date": date_range,

    "Sales": sales

})
df.set_index("Date", inplace=True)


# Calculate a 3-month rolling average to smooth out fluctuations
df["Rolling_Avg"] = df["Sales"].rolling(window=3).mean()


# Plot the sales data and the rolling average trend
plt.figure(figsize=(10, 5))

plt.plot(df.index, df["Sales"], label="Monthly Sales", marker="o")

plt.plot(df.index, df["Rolling_Avg"], label="3-Month Rolling Average",
linestyle="--")

plt.title("Market Trend Analysis: Monthly Sales")

plt.xlabel("Date")
```

```python
plt.ylabel("Sales")

plt.legend()

plt.grid(True)

plt.show()
```

Explanation:

- **Data Simulation:**
  A dataset is generated to simulate monthly sales over a two-year period.
- **Rolling Average:**
  A 3-month rolling average is calculated to smooth short-term fluctuations and highlight long-term trends.
- **Visualization:**
  The plot displays both raw sales data and the rolling average, providing insights that can inform strategic decisions.

10.2. Enhancing Decision-Making with Autonomous Insights

Overview

Autonomous insights refer to the ability of agentic AI systems to analyze data continuously and generate actionable recommendations. These insights enhance decision-making by providing real-time, evidence-based input to human strategists, thereby reducing uncertainty and improving operational responsiveness.

Key Benefits of Autonomous Insights:

1. **Real-Time Analytics:**
   - **Function:**
     Continuous data monitoring allows for immediate identification of opportunities and risks.
   - **Impact:**
     Facilitates rapid decision-making and timely interventions, critical in fast-changing markets.
2. **Data-Driven Recommendations:**

- ○ **Function:**
  AI models synthesize complex data to offer recommendations that are often beyond the scope of traditional analysis.
- ○ **Impact:**
  Empowers leaders with actionable insights, such as adjusting marketing campaigns or reallocating resources.

3. **Scenario Analysis and Simulation:**
   - ○ **Function:**
     Autonomous systems can simulate various scenarios to predict the outcomes of different strategic decisions.
   - ○ **Impact:**
     Supports robust planning by evaluating potential risks and benefits before implementation.

4. **Reducing Cognitive Load:**
   - ○ **Function:**
     By automating data analysis, AI frees executives from routine tasks, allowing them to focus on high-level strategy.
   - ○ **Impact:**
     Enhances overall productivity and ensures that decisions are made based on comprehensive, up-to-date information.

Table: Enhancing Decision-Making with Autonomous Insights

Aspect	Description	Impact on Decision-Making
Real-Time Analytics	Continuous monitoring of key performance indicators (KPIs).	Immediate detection of trends and issues, enabling swift action.
Data-Driven Recommendations	AI generates suggestions based on aggregated and analyzed data.	Informed and objective decision-making with reduced bias.

Scenario Analysis	Simulation of various strategies and their potential outcomes.	Better risk management and strategic planning.
Cognitive Load Reduction	Automates routine data processing and analysis.	Allows decision-makers to focus on strategic, high-impact issues.

Example: Autonomous Insights for Resource Allocation

Below is a Python code example that simulates an autonomous system recommending resource allocation based on real-time performance metrics. This simplified example uses a basic rule-based approach to decide whether to increase, decrease, or maintain current resource levels.

python

```python
import random


def generate_performance_metric():
    """
    Simulate a performance metric (e.g., revenue growth percentage).
    """
    return random.uniform(-10, 10)  # Simulated percentage change


def autonomous_resource_decision(performance):
    """
    Determine resource allocation based on performance metric.
```

- If performance > 5%, recommend increasing resources.

- If performance < -5%, recommend reducing resources.

- Otherwise, maintain current levels.

"""

```python
if performance > 5:

    return "Increase Resources"

elif performance < -5:

    return "Reduce Resources"

else:

    return "Maintain Resources"


# Simulate real-time decision-making over 5 cycles

print("Autonomous Resource Allocation Decisions:")

for cycle in range(5):

    performance_metric = generate_performance_metric()

    decision = autonomous_resource_decision(performance_metric)

    print(f"Cycle {cycle+1}: Performance = {performance_metric:.2f}% ->
Decision: {decision}")
```

Explanation:

- **Performance Metric Simulation:**
  The function generate_performance_metric simulates a percentage change in performance, representing metrics such as revenue growth.
- **Decision Logic:**
  The autonomous_resource_decision function provides recommendations based on the simulated performance. If performance exceeds 5%, the system suggests

increasing resources; if performance drops below -5%, it recommends reducing resources; otherwise, it suggests maintaining current levels.

- **Outcome:**
  The simulation runs over multiple cycles, showing how autonomous insights can lead to dynamic, data-driven decisions in resource management.

Agentic AI plays a transformative role in business strategy by enabling rapid, data-driven decision-making. In section 10.1, we explored how AI influences business strategy by analyzing market trends, optimizing operations, and managing risks. Section 10.2 demonstrated how autonomous insights, driven by real-time analytics and scenario simulation, enhance decision-making processes, reduce cognitive load, and support strategic agility.

By integrating these technologies and processes, organizations can achieve a competitive edge, adapt to market changes swiftly, and make more informed, transparent decisions that drive long-term success.

10.3. Blending Human Judgment with AI Analytics

Overview

While AI analytics offer powerful data-driven insights, they can sometimes lack the context, intuition, and ethical considerations that human judgment brings. Blending human expertise with AI analytics creates a hybrid decision-making framework. This approach leverages the computational power and pattern recognition capabilities of AI while incorporating the nuanced, experience-based insights of human decision-makers.

Key Elements of the Hybrid Approach

1. **Complementary Strengths:**
   - **AI Analytics:**
     - Processes large volumes of data rapidly.
     - Identifies patterns, trends, and anomalies that may be difficult for humans to discern.
     - Provides predictive insights based on historical data.
   - **Human Judgment:**
     - Applies contextual understanding and ethical considerations.
     - Interprets complex situations where ambiguity exists.
     - Considers external factors and strategic nuances that data alone may not capture.
2. **Decision Augmentation:**

- **Process:**
  AI systems generate recommendations or predictions, and human experts review these outputs to add context or override decisions when necessary.
- **Benefits:**
  - Improves overall decision quality.
  - Reduces risks associated with over-reliance on automated processes.
  - Ensures accountability and ethical oversight.

3. **Iterative Feedback Loops:**
   - **Human Feedback:**
     - Human experts provide feedback on AI predictions, which is then used to refine and retrain models.
   - **Continuous Improvement:**
     - This collaborative loop ensures that the AI system evolves and aligns more closely with organizational values and real-world conditions.

Comparative Table: AI-Only vs. Human Judgment vs. Hybrid Decision-Making

Aspect	AI-Only	Human Judgment	Hybrid (AI + Human)
Speed	Very fast, processes large datasets quickly	Slower, relies on experience and analysis	Fast processing with contextual oversight
Data Processing	Excellent at handling and analyzing quantitative data	Limited to available data and personal experience	Combines quantitative insights with qualitative context
Ethical Considerations	May miss ethical nuances or context	Can incorporate ethical and cultural considerations	Balances ethical oversight with data-driven decisions

Adaptability	Continuously learns from historical data	Adapts based on changing scenarios and intuition	Iterative feedback improves model accuracy and relevance
Decision Quality	Highly consistent but may lack context	Rich in context but can be biased or inconsistent	Enhanced decision quality through complementary strengths

Example: Integrating Human Judgment in a Financial Decision

Consider a scenario where an AI system forecasts market trends and recommends investment strategies. While the AI might identify a statistically significant trend, a human analyst can evaluate external factors such as geopolitical events or emerging regulatory changes that the model may not account for. The final decision reflects both the AI's quantitative analysis and the human's qualitative insights.

Simplified Python Example

The following code illustrates a basic simulation where an AI model predicts a recommendation, and then a human expert adjusts that recommendation based on additional context.

python

```
import random


def ai_recommendation(market_data):
    """

    Simulate an AI recommendation based on market data.

    For this example, if the average market indicator is above a threshold,
recommend 'Invest More';
```

```python
    otherwise, recommend 'Hold'.
    """

    avg_indicator = sum(market_data) / len(market_data)

    return "Invest More" if avg_indicator > 0.5 else "Hold"


def human_adjustment(ai_rec, external_context):
    """

    Simulate human judgment adjusting the AI recommendation.

    If external context is unfavorable (e.g., high geopolitical risk), override to
'Hold' even if AI recommends 'Invest More'.

    """

    if external_context == "High Risk":

        return "Hold"

    return ai_rec


# Simulated market data and external context

market_data = [random.uniform(0, 1) for _ in range(10)]

external_context = random.choice(["Low Risk", "High Risk"])


# AI generates a recommendation

ai_rec = ai_recommendation(market_data)

print(f"AI Recommendation: {ai_rec}")


# Human expert reviews and adjusts the recommendation
```

```
final_decision = human_adjustment(ai_rec, external_context)

print(f"External Context: {external_context}")

print(f"Final Decision after Human Judgment: {final_decision}")
```

Explanation:

- **AI Recommendation:**
  The ai_recommendation function computes the average of simulated market data and issues a recommendation based on a threshold.
- **Human Adjustment:**
  The human_adjustment function simulates a scenario where human expertise adjusts the AI's recommendation if external factors indicate high risk.
- **Outcome:**
  The final decision reflects a blend of AI analytics and human judgment, ensuring that strategic decisions are both data-driven and contextually aware.

10.4. Strategic Case Studies and Learning Outcomes

Overview

Strategic case studies provide concrete examples of how organizations blend human judgment with AI analytics to drive innovation and achieve competitive advantages. These case studies offer valuable lessons on best practices, challenges, and measurable outcomes. In this section, we outline strategic case studies from various industries and detail the learning outcomes derived from these real-world examples.

Components of a Strategic Case Study

Each case study typically covers the following aspects:

1. **Background and Context:**
   - **Overview:**
     Description of the industry, the specific business challenge, and the strategic goals.
   - **Stakeholders:**
     Identification of key players involved, such as management teams, AI experts, and external partners.

2. **Implementation Process:**
   - **Technology and Tools:**
     Details on the AI platforms, algorithms, and integration techniques used.
   - **Workflow Integration:**
     How the AI system was incorporated into existing processes and how human judgment was integrated.
   - **Challenges and Resolutions:**
     Key obstacles encountered and strategies used to overcome them.
3. **Results and Impact:**
   - **Quantitative Outcomes:**
     Metrics such as cost savings, revenue growth, efficiency improvements, or risk reduction.
   - **Qualitative Insights:**
     Feedback from stakeholders, customer satisfaction, and broader strategic benefits.
4. **Lessons Learned:**
   - **Best Practices:**
     Insights into what worked well and recommendations for similar future projects.
   - **Areas for Improvement:**
     Identification of challenges that remain and suggestions for further refinement.

Case Study Example: Retail Marketing Optimization

Background:
A mid-sized retail company sought to improve its digital marketing efforts by leveraging AI to analyze customer behavior and optimize advertising campaigns. The goal was to increase customer engagement and drive sales growth while balancing data-driven insights with human creativity.

Implementation Process:

- **Technology Stack:**
  - **Data Sources:** Website analytics, social media engagement, and transaction records.
  - **AI Models:** Predictive analytics and recommendation algorithms developed using TensorFlow.
  - **Human Integration:** Marketing experts reviewed AI-generated insights and adjusted campaign strategies based on brand guidelines and customer feedback.
- **Workflow Integration:**

- ○ **Data Collection:** Automated pipelines gathered data in real time.
- ○ **Analysis:** The AI system identified customer segments and predicted the most effective advertising channels.
- ○ **Execution:** Marketing teams implemented campaigns based on AI recommendations, with ongoing adjustments informed by human judgment.
- **Challenges:**
  - ○ **Data Quality:** Ensuring data accuracy across diverse sources.
  - ○ **Interpretability:** Translating complex AI insights into actionable marketing strategies.
  - ○ **Collaboration:** Achieving seamless integration between technical teams and marketing professionals.
- **Results and Impact:**
  - ○ **Quantitative Outcomes:** 25% increase in click-through rates and 15% boost in sales over six months.
  - ○ **Qualitative Insights:** Improved customer engagement and positive feedback on personalized marketing efforts.

Lessons Learned:

- **Best Practices:**
  - ○ Integrate data pipelines with real-time analytics.
  - ○ Foster collaboration between AI experts and marketing teams.
  - ○ Invest in explainable AI to make insights accessible.
- **Areas for Improvement:**
  - ○ Enhance data cleaning processes.
  - ○ Further train staff on interpreting AI outputs.
  - ○ Develop iterative feedback loops to refine models continuously.

Learning Outcomes Table

Learning Outcome	Description
Understanding Integration:	Learn how to combine AI analytics with human expertise to enhance decision-making.

Practical Implementation: Gain insights into real-world processes for integrating AI into existing workflows.

Measuring Impact: Understand key metrics and methods to evaluate the success of AI-driven strategies.

Overcoming Challenges: Identify common obstacles in blending AI with human judgment and explore practical solutions.

Strategic Innovation: Develop strategies for leveraging AI to drive innovation while maintaining human oversight.

Summary

Blending human judgment with AI analytics leads to more informed, adaptable, and ethically sound strategic decisions. Strategic case studies illustrate real-world implementations, challenges, and successes across various industries. By studying these examples, organizations can learn best practices for integrating AI into their decision-making processes, measure the impact of these initiatives, and refine their approaches over time.

Chapter 11 Troubleshooting and Optimizing Agentic AI

Agentic AI systems are designed to function autonomously in dynamic environments. However, like any complex system, they may encounter challenges that can affect performance, reliability, and efficiency. This section provides an in-depth discussion on common challenges and practical techniques for troubleshooting and optimizing these systems.

11.1. Common Challenges and How to Overcome Them

Agentic AI systems can face several challenges during development and deployment. Understanding these common issues and knowing how to address them is critical for maintaining robust, reliable, and efficient operations.

Common Challenges

1. **Sensor Noise and Inaccurate Data:**
   - **Issue:**
     Sensor inputs are often noisy or subject to error, leading to inaccurate perceptions of the environment.
   - **Solutions:**
     - **Filtering Techniques:** Apply smoothing algorithms such as Kalman filters or moving averages.
     - **Redundancy:** Use multiple sensors for the same input and aggregate the data to improve accuracy.
2. **Overfitting and Poor Generalization:**
   - **Issue:**
     Models may perform well on training data but fail to generalize to new, unseen data.
   - **Solutions:**
     - **Regularization:** Techniques such as L1 or L2 regularization help prevent overfitting.
     - **Cross-Validation:** Use k-fold cross-validation to ensure the model generalizes well.
     - **Data Augmentation:** Increase the diversity of the training set by augmenting data.
3. **Latency and Real-Time Constraints:**

- o **Issue:**

  Autonomous systems often need to process data and make decisions in real time, but high computational demands can introduce latency.
- o **Solutions:**
  - **Model Optimization:** Simplify models or use quantization techniques.
  - **Hardware Acceleration:** Leverage GPUs, TPUs, or dedicated hardware accelerators.
  - **Efficient Algorithms:** Employ algorithms with lower computational complexity.

4. **System Integration and Communication Errors:**
   - o **Issue:**

     In complex systems, integrating different components (e.g., sensors, models, actuators) can lead to communication failures or misalignment.
   - o **Solutions:**
     - **Robust Middleware:** Use reliable communication protocols and middleware.
     - **Modular Testing:** Test each component independently before full integration.
     - **Error Logging:** Implement comprehensive logging and monitoring to quickly identify issues.

5. **Adaptability and Learning Rate Issues:**
   - o **Issue:**

     Autonomous agents must adapt to changing conditions. A model that learns too slowly may not respond adequately to new situations, while one that learns too quickly may become unstable.
   - o **Solutions:**
     - **Adaptive Learning Rates:** Use algorithms like Adam or RMSprop that adjust learning rates dynamically.
     - **Feedback Loops:** Implement feedback mechanisms that allow the agent to learn continuously and adjust parameters accordingly.

Comparative Table: Common Challenges and Solutions

Challenge	Description	Potential Solutions

Sensor Noise	Erroneous or inconsistent sensor data	Filtering (Kalman filter, moving average), sensor redundancy
Overfitting	Model performs well on training data but poorly on new data	Regularization (L1/L2), cross-validation, data augmentation
Latency	Delays in processing due to high computational demand	Model optimization, hardware acceleration, efficient algorithms
System Integration Errors	Communication failures between components	Robust middleware, modular testing, comprehensive logging
Adaptability and Learning Rate	Inadequate adaptation to new conditions	Adaptive learning rates, continuous feedback loops, parameter tuning

11.2. Techniques for Performance Tuning and Efficiency

Optimizing the performance of agentic AI systems is an ongoing process that involves fine-tuning model parameters, optimizing computational resources, and ensuring smooth integration of system components. Below are several techniques and best practices to enhance performance and efficiency.

Techniques for Performance Tuning

1. **Hyperparameter Tuning:**
   - **Definition:**
     Adjusting model hyperparameters (e.g., learning rate, number of layers, batch size) to achieve optimal performance.

- **Techniques:**
  - **Grid Search:** Exhaustively searches a specified parameter space.
  - **Random Search:** Samples a wide range of hyperparameter combinations randomly.
  - **Bayesian Optimization:** Uses probabilistic models to find optimal parameters more efficiently.
- **Example:**
  Using scikit-learn's GridSearchCV for model tuning.

2. **Model Simplification and Pruning:**
   - **Definition:**
     Reducing the complexity of the model to improve computational efficiency without significantly impacting performance.
   - **Techniques:**
     - **Pruning:** Removing redundant nodes or layers from a neural network.
     - **Quantization:** Reducing the precision of the model parameters to lower computational overhead.
     - **Knowledge Distillation:** Training a smaller model (student) to replicate the performance of a larger model (teacher).

3. **Algorithm Optimization:**
   - **Definition:**
     Choosing or designing algorithms that are computationally efficient.
   - **Techniques:**
     - **Parallel Processing:** Distribute computations across multiple cores or GPUs.
     - **Algorithmic Improvements:** Use more efficient data structures or algorithms with lower time complexity.

4. **Hardware Utilization:**
   - **Definition:**
     Leveraging specialized hardware to accelerate model training and inference.
   - **Techniques:**
     - **GPUs/TPUs:** Utilize graphics processing units or tensor processing units for faster computation.
     - **Edge Computing:** Process data closer to the source to reduce latency.

Techniques for Enhancing Efficiency

1. **Batch Processing:**

- o **Definition:**

  Processing data in batches rather than one sample at a time to utilize computational resources more effectively.
- o **Benefits:**
  - Reduces overhead and improves throughput.
  - Allows for more efficient use of memory and parallel processing.

2. **Caching and Data Preprocessing:**
   - o **Definition:**

     Storing intermediate results or preprocessed data to avoid redundant computations.
   - o **Benefits:**
     - Speeds up repeated data access.
     - Reduces computational overhead during model inference.

3. **Profiling and Monitoring:**
   - o **Definition:**

     Continuously monitoring system performance to identify bottlenecks.
   - o **Tools:**
     - **Profilers:** Use Python's cProfile, TensorBoard, or other monitoring tools to analyze performance.
     - **Logging:** Implement detailed logs to track runtime performance and error rates.

Example: Hyperparameter Tuning with GridSearchCV

Below is a Python code example that demonstrates how to use GridSearchCV from scikit-learn to tune hyperparameters for a simple classifier.

python

```python
import numpy as np

from sklearn.datasets import load_iris

from sklearn.model_selection import train_test_split, GridSearchCV

from sklearn.ensemble import RandomForestClassifier

from sklearn.metrics import accuracy_score
```

```python
# Load the Iris dataset
iris = load_iris()

X = iris.data

y = iris.target


# Split the dataset into training and test sets
X_train, X_test, y_train, y_test = train_test_split(X, y, test_size=0.2, random_state=42)


# Define a RandomForestClassifier and a parameter grid for tuning
clf = RandomForestClassifier(random_state=42)

param_grid = {
    'n_estimators': [50, 100, 150],
    'max_depth': [None, 5, 10],
    'min_samples_split': [2, 4, 6]
}


# Perform grid search with cross-validation
grid_search = GridSearchCV(estimator=clf, param_grid=param_grid, cv=5, scoring='accuracy')

grid_search.fit(X_train, y_train)


# Best parameters and corresponding accuracy
best_params = grid_search.best_params_
```

```
best_model = grid_search.best_estimator_

y_pred = best_model.predict(X_test)

accuracy = accuracy_score(y_test, y_pred)


print("Best Parameters:", best_params)

print("Test Accuracy:", accuracy)
```

Explanation:

- **Dataset and Model:**
  The Iris dataset is loaded and split into training and test sets. A RandomForestClassifier is defined as the base model.
- **Parameter Grid:**
  A dictionary specifies various values for hyperparameters such as n_estimators, max_depth, and min_samples_split.
- **Grid Search:**
  GridSearchCV performs exhaustive search over the parameter grid using 5-fold cross-validation to determine the best parameters.
- **Results:**
  The best hyperparameters and the corresponding test accuracy are printed, showcasing the impact of hyperparameter tuning on model performance.

Comparative Table: Optimization Techniques

Technique	Description	Benefits
Hyperparameter Tuning	Adjusting parameters (e.g., learning rate, depth) using search methods	Improved model accuracy and generalization

Model Pruning and Quantization	Reducing model complexity and precision to optimize computation	Lower computational cost and faster inference
Batch Processing	Processing data in batches rather than one at a time	Increased throughput and better resource utilization
Hardware Acceleration	Using GPUs/TPUs to speed up computations	Significant reduction in training and inference time
Profiling and Monitoring	Using tools to analyze performance and identify bottlenecks	Enhanced troubleshooting and targeted optimization

Summary

In summary, troubleshooting and optimizing agentic AI involves identifying common challenges—such as sensor noise, overfitting, latency, integration errors, and adaptability issues—and applying targeted solutions such as filtering, regularization, adaptive learning, and hardware acceleration. Performance tuning techniques, including hyperparameter tuning, model simplification, algorithm optimization, and efficient resource utilization, play a vital role in ensuring that AI systems perform effectively and efficiently.

By employing these strategies and using tools like GridSearchCV for hyperparameter tuning, developers can enhance the reliability, speed, and accuracy of their agentic AI systems while ensuring robust performance in dynamic real-world environments.

This detailed explanation, supported by practical examples and comparative tables, provides a clear roadmap for troubleshooting and optimizing agentic AI systems in a professional and accessible manner.

11.3. Scalability and Maintenance Best Practices

Overview

As agentic AI systems grow in complexity and scale, ensuring that they remain efficient, reliable, and maintainable over time is essential. Scalability refers to the system's ability to handle increased loads or data volumes without performance degradation, while maintenance encompasses regular updates, bug fixes, and performance monitoring. Together, scalability and maintenance best practices help ensure the longevity and robustness of an AI system.

Best Practices for Scalability

1. **Modular Architecture:**
   - **Description:**
     Design the system as a collection of independent modules (e.g., data ingestion, processing, decision-making, actuation) that can be scaled independently.
   - **Benefits:**
     - Easier to update and maintain.
     - Allows targeted scaling of high-demand components.
   - **Example:**
     Using microservices to separate data processing from decision-making logic.
2. **Load Balancing and Distributed Computing:**
   - **Description:**
     Distribute workloads across multiple servers or nodes using load balancers.
   - **Benefits:**
     - Reduces latency.
     - Ensures high availability and fault tolerance.
   - **Example:**
     Deploying AI services on a cloud platform with autoscaling features.
3. **Efficient Data Management:**
   - **Description:**
     Optimize data storage and retrieval using databases, caching mechanisms, and data pipelines.
   - **Benefits:**
     - Improves response times.
     - Reduces overhead during high-load periods.

- Example:
  Using NoSQL databases for real-time data ingestion and in-memory caches (e.g., Redis) to speed up data access.

4. **Scalable Infrastructure:**
   - **Description:**
     Leverage cloud-based services and containerization (e.g., Docker, Kubernetes) to manage infrastructure.
   - **Benefits:**
     - Enables seamless scaling up or down based on demand.
     - Simplifies deployment and maintenance.
   - **Example:**
     Deploying the AI system on cloud platforms like AWS, Azure, or Google Cloud.

Best Practices for Maintenance

1. **Regular Monitoring and Logging:**
   - **Description:**
     Implement comprehensive logging and monitoring to detect performance issues, errors, and anomalies.
   - **Benefits:**
     - Facilitates proactive troubleshooting.
     - Provides insights into system health and usage patterns.
   - **Tools:**
     - Monitoring tools: Prometheus, Grafana.
     - Logging tools: ELK Stack (Elasticsearch, Logstash, Kibana).

2. **Automated Testing and Continuous Integration/Continuous Deployment (CI/CD):**
   - **Description:**
     Use automated tests and CI/CD pipelines to ensure that updates do not introduce new issues.
   - **Benefits:**
     - Increases reliability.
     - Reduces downtime during updates.
   - **Example:**
     Running unit, integration, and end-to-end tests automatically on each code commit.

3. **Regular Updates and Patch Management:**
   - **Description:**
     Keep libraries, frameworks, and system components up to date.
   - **Benefits:**

- Enhances security.
- Improves performance and compatibility.
- **Example:**
Scheduling regular maintenance windows to update dependencies and apply security patches.
4. **Documentation and Knowledge Sharing:**
   - **Description:**
Maintain thorough documentation on system architecture, configurations, and operational procedures.
   - **Benefits:**
      - Simplifies troubleshooting and onboarding of new team members.
      - Provides a reference for best practices.
   - **Example:**
Using wikis or internal documentation platforms to keep records up to date.

Comparative Table: Scalability and Maintenance Best Practices

Area	Best Practice	Benefits	Example Tools/Approaches
Architecture	Modular and microservices design	Easier scaling, targeted updates	Docker, Kubernetes
Load Balancing	Distribute workloads across multiple nodes	Reduces latency, improves fault tolerance	Nginx, AWS Elastic Load Balancing
Data Management	Efficient storage, caching, and pipelines	Faster data access, reduced overhead	NoSQL databases, Redis

Infrastructure	Cloud-based deployment and autoscaling	Seamless scaling, flexible resource management	AWS, Azure, Google Cloud
Monitoring & Logging	Continuous monitoring and detailed logs	Proactive troubleshooting, insights into system health	Prometheus, Grafana, ELK Stack
Testing & CI/CD	Automated tests and deployment pipelines	Reduced downtime, improved reliability	Jenkins, GitLab CI, Travis CI
Updates & Patches	Regular maintenance and dependency updates	Enhanced security and performance	Scheduled maintenance windows
Documentation	Comprehensive and accessible documentation	Simplified troubleshooting, effective knowledge transfer	Confluence, internal wikis

11.4. Interactive Q&A: Diagnosing and Fixing Issues

Overview

Interactive Q&A sessions are an effective way to diagnose and fix issues in agentic AI systems. They provide a structured format for troubleshooting, enabling both technical teams and stakeholders to understand problems, identify root causes, and apply solutions. Interactive Q&A can be implemented through forums, chatbots, or even command-line interfaces that guide users through diagnostic steps.

Key Components of an Interactive Q&A System

1. **Question Repository:**
   - **Description:**
     A database or knowledge base that stores common issues, troubleshooting steps, and best practices.
   - **Benefits:**
     - Quick access to solutions.
     - Continuous improvement as new issues are documented.
   - **Example:**
     A FAQ section on an internal website or a chatbot trained on support documents.
2. **Diagnostic Workflow:**
   - **Description:**
     A guided process that asks users specific questions to narrow down potential issues.
   - **Benefits:**
     - Helps in systematically identifying the problem.
     - Reduces guesswork and speeds up resolution.
   - **Example:**
     An interactive script that prompts users to check sensor status, data logs, and performance metrics.
3. **Automated Recommendations:**
   - **Description:**
     Based on the answers provided, the system suggests likely solutions or next steps.
   - **Benefits:**
     - Offers immediate support.
     - Can integrate with ticketing systems to escalate unresolved issues.
   - **Example:**
     A diagnostic tool that suggests restarting services, applying patches, or reviewing configuration files.

Example: Interactive Q&A Script for Diagnosing Issues

Below is a Python script that simulates an interactive Q&A session for diagnosing common issues in an agentic AI system. This script uses a simple question-and-answer format to guide the user through troubleshooting steps.

python

```python
def interactive_qna():

    print("Welcome to the Agentic AI Diagnostic Tool!")

    print("Please answer the following questions to help diagnose the
issue.\n")


    # Step 1: Check Sensor Data

    sensor_status = input("Are all sensors reporting data correctly? (yes/no):
").strip().lower()

    if sensor_status == "no":

        print("Recommendation: Check sensor connections and calibration.
Consider applying a filtering technique.")

        return


    # Step 2: Check System Logs

    logs_status = input("Are there any error messages in the system logs?
(yes/no): ").strip().lower()

    if logs_status == "yes":

        print("Recommendation: Review the logs for error codes and consult
the troubleshooting guide for specific errors.")

        return


    # Step 3: Performance Metrics

    performance_issue = input("Is the system experiencing high latency or
slow responses? (yes/no): ").strip().lower()

    if performance_issue == "yes":
```

```python
        print("Recommendation: Consider optimizing the model or using
hardware acceleration (e.g., GPUs/TPUs) to improve performance.")

        return


    # Step 4: Model Accuracy

    accuracy_issue = input("Is the AI model performing poorly on new data?
(yes/no): ").strip().lower()

    if accuracy_issue == "yes":

        print("Recommendation: Check for overfitting. Use cross-validation,
regularization, or data augmentation to improve model generalization.")

        return


    # If all answers are 'no'

    print("It appears that the system is operating normally. If you continue to
experience issues, please consult with your technical team or escalate the
ticket.")


if __name__ == "__main__":

    interactive_qna()
```

Explanation:

- **Interactive Session:**
  The script begins with a welcome message and then prompts the user with a
  series of questions regarding common issues like sensor data, system logs,
  performance, and model accuracy.
- **Decision Logic:**
  Depending on the user's responses, the script provides specific
  recommendations. If the user indicates a problem at any step, the script outputs
  an appropriate troubleshooting recommendation and exits.

- **Outcome:**
  This interactive tool helps users systematically diagnose issues and suggests actionable solutions.

Best Practices for Interactive Q&A Systems

- **User-Friendly Interface:**
  Ensure that the Q&A system is intuitive, with clear and simple language that guides users step by step.
- **Comprehensive Coverage:**
  Regularly update the repository of questions and solutions to cover emerging issues and new features.
- **Integration with Support Systems:**
  Connect the interactive tool with a ticketing system or support portal so unresolved issues can be escalated efficiently.
- **Feedback Loop:**
  Incorporate user feedback to continually improve the diagnostic process and update the knowledge base.

Summary

- **Scalability and Maintenance Best Practices:**
  Implementing modular architecture, load balancing, efficient data management, and robust monitoring ensures that agentic AI systems remain scalable and maintainable. Regular testing, updates, and documentation further enhance long-term reliability.
- **Interactive Q&A for Troubleshooting:**
  An interactive Q&A system helps diagnose and fix common issues through guided, step-by-step troubleshooting. Such systems leverage automated recommendations and comprehensive knowledge bases to reduce downtime and improve system performance.

By following these guidelines and leveraging interactive tools, organizations can maintain high-performance, scalable agentic AI systems and quickly address any operational issues that arise.

Chapter 12 Interactive Tools, Exercises, and Hands-On Projects

In the context of agentic AI, interactive tools and hands-on projects are essential for transforming theoretical knowledge into practical skills. They serve as invaluable resources for reinforcing learning, testing concepts, and speeding up the development process. This section outlines the role of cheat sheets, templates, and quick guides as well as practical exercises designed for each chapter.

12.1. Cheat Sheets, Templates, and Quick Guides

Overview

Cheat sheets, templates, and quick guides are concise, accessible resources that provide quick references to essential concepts, commands, and processes. They are particularly useful when learning new technologies or workflows, as they help consolidate complex information into an easy-to-digest format.

Key Characteristics and Benefits:

1. **Cheat Sheets:**
   - **Purpose:**
     Provide compact summaries of key information such as syntax, commands, algorithms, and workflows.
   - **Benefits:**
     - Quick lookup for essential commands or parameters.
     - Aids in memorization and reinforces learning.
   - **Example Topics:**
     - Common Python commands for data manipulation.
     - Key functions in TensorFlow or PyTorch.
     - Standard performance metrics in AI.
2. **Templates:**
   - **Purpose:**
     Offer pre-structured code or project frameworks that can be customized for specific tasks.
   - **Benefits:**
     - Reduces development time by providing a ready-made structure.
     - Ensures consistency across projects.

- Useful for standard processes like data preprocessing, model training, and evaluation.
  - **Example Templates:**
    - A template for a neural network model using Keras.
    - A data pipeline template for preprocessing and feature engineering.
    - A standard project structure for agentic AI systems.
3. **Quick Guides:**
   - **Purpose:**
   Present step-by-step instructions for completing tasks or troubleshooting common issues.
   - **Benefits:**
     - Streamlines the learning process.
     - Provides a clear pathway from problem identification to solution.
   - **Example Topics:**
     - Setting up a virtual environment for AI development.
     - Deploying an AI model to production.
     - Using debugging tools to diagnose performance issues.

Table: Example Quick Reference Guide for Agentic AI Development

Section	Content	Example/Action
Environment Setup	Commands to create and activate virtual environments	python -m venv env source env/bin/activate
Data Preprocessing	Steps for cleaning and scaling data	Use pandas for cleaning, StandardScaler for normalization
Model Training	Key parameters and commands for training a model	model.fit(X_train, y_train, epochs=50, batch_size=32)

Evaluation	Common metrics and visualization techniques	Accuracy, confusion matrix, ROC curve visualization
Troubleshooting	Common error messages and quick fixes	Check sensor connections, verify data formats, update dependencies

Example: Python Code for a Basic Cheat Sheet Generator

Below is a simple Python script that creates a cheat sheet for frequently used commands in a typical agentic AI project. This script can be easily extended or modified as needed.

python

```python
def display_cheat_sheet():
    cheat_sheet = {
        "Environment Setup": [
            "python -m venv env",
            "source env/bin/activate (Linux/Mac) or env\\Scripts\\activate (Windows)",
            "pip install --upgrade pip"
        ],
        "Data Preprocessing": [
            "import pandas as pd",
            "df = pd.read_csv('data.csv')",
            "df.fillna(method='ffill', inplace=True)",
            "from sklearn.preprocessing import StandardScaler",
```

```python
        "scaler = StandardScaler()",

        "df_scaled = scaler.fit_transform(df)"

    ],

    "Model Training (Keras)": [

        "from tensorflow.keras.models import Sequential",

        "from tensorflow.keras.layers import Dense",

        "model = Sequential([Dense(10, activation='relu',
input_shape=(n_features,)), Dense(1, activation='sigmoid')])",

        "model.compile(optimizer='adam', loss='binary_crossentropy',
metrics=['accuracy'])",

        "model.fit(X_train, y_train, epochs=50, batch_size=32)"

    ],

    "Evaluation": [

        "loss, accuracy = model.evaluate(X_test, y_test)",

        "print(f'Test Accuracy: {accuracy:.2f}')"

    ]

}


for section, commands in cheat_sheet.items():

    print(f"\n{section}:")

    for cmd in commands:

        print(f"  - {cmd}")


if __name__ == "__main__":
```

Explanation:

- **Structure:**
  The cheat sheet is organized as a dictionary with keys representing sections and values as lists of relevant commands or code snippets.
- **Display Function:**
  The display_cheat_sheet() function iterates over the dictionary and prints out the information in a structured format.
- **Customization:**
  This basic structure can be expanded to include more sections, examples, or even interactive prompts.

12.2. Practical Exercises for Each Chapter

Overview

Practical exercises are hands-on projects or tasks designed to reinforce the concepts covered in each chapter. They encourage active learning by allowing readers to apply theoretical knowledge to real-world scenarios. Exercises can range from simple coding challenges to comprehensive projects that mimic real-life applications.

Benefits of Practical Exercises:

1. **Reinforcement of Learning:**
   - Exercises help consolidate concepts by providing practical application opportunities.
   - They enable learners to experiment, make mistakes, and learn through experience.
2. **Skill Development:**
   - Hands-on projects enhance technical skills, such as coding, debugging, and system integration.
   - They promote problem-solving and critical thinking.
3. **Real-World Relevance:**
   - Practical exercises simulate real-world challenges, preparing learners for professional applications.
   - They illustrate how to use tools and techniques in context.
4. **Feedback and Iteration:**

- ○ Working through exercises allows learners to receive feedback—either from peers, mentors, or automated systems—which is essential for continuous improvement.

Structure of Practical Exercises:

Each practical exercise can include:

- **Objective:**
  A clear statement of what the exercise aims to achieve.
- **Instructions:**
  Step-by-step guidelines on how to complete the exercise.
- **Starter Code:**
  A code template that provides a foundation for the task.
- **Expected Outcome:**
  Description of what a successful solution looks like.
- **Reflection Questions:**
  Questions that prompt learners to consider what worked, what didn't, and how the solution could be improved.

Example Table: Practical Exercise Outline for a Chapter

Exercise Element	Description	Example
Objective	Define the goal of the exercise.	"Build a simple data preprocessing pipeline using pandas."
Instructions	Step-by-step guide to complete the task.	"Load data, handle missing values, and scale features."
Starter Code	Provide a template to get started.	See code snippet for a basic pandas pipeline.

| Expected Outcome | Define the deliverable or result. | "A cleaned and normalized dataset ready for model training." |
| Reflection Questions | Questions to encourage deeper thinking. | "How did handling missing data affect the results?" |

Example: Practical Exercise Code for Data Preprocessing

Below is a sample exercise that guides the learner through building a data preprocessing pipeline. This exercise reinforces the concepts of data cleaning, handling missing values, and feature scaling.

python

```python
import pandas as pd

from sklearn.preprocessing import StandardScaler

from sklearn.impute import SimpleImputer


def load_and_preprocess_data(file_path):
    """
    Objective:
        - Load a dataset from a CSV file.

        - Handle missing values by imputing the mean.

        - Scale numerical features using StandardScaler.


    Instructions:
        1. Read the CSV file into a pandas DataFrame.
```

2. Identify and impute missing values in numeric columns.

3. Scale the numeric columns.

4. Return the preprocessed DataFrame.

Expected Outcome:

- A DataFrame with no missing values and scaled features.

"""

```python
# Step 1: Load data
df = pd.read_csv(file_path)
print("Original Data:")
print(df.head())


# Step 2: Identify numeric columns for preprocessing
numeric_cols = df.select_dtypes(include=['float64', 'int64']).columns


# Step 3: Handle missing values using mean imputation
imputer = SimpleImputer(strategy='mean')
df[numeric_cols] = imputer.fit_transform(df[numeric_cols])


# Step 4: Scale numeric features using StandardScaler
scaler = StandardScaler()
df[numeric_cols] = scaler.fit_transform(df[numeric_cols])
```

```
print("\nPreprocessed Data:")

print(df.head())

return df


# Example usage:

if __name__ == "__main__":

    # Assume 'sample_data.csv' is a CSV file in the current directory

    preprocessed_df = load_and_preprocess_data("sample_data.csv")
```

Explanation:

- **Objective:**
  The function's docstring clearly states the exercise's objectives and expected outcomes.
- **Instructions:**
  Step-by-step instructions are provided within the docstring.
- **Starter Code:**
  The code template reads data, imputes missing values, scales features, and prints the before-and-after states of the data.
- **Expected Outcome:**
  The learner should end up with a DataFrame that has no missing values and scaled numeric features.
- **Reflection:**
  Learners can consider how different imputation strategies or scaling methods might affect the model's performance.

Summary

- **Cheat Sheets, Templates, and Quick Guides:**
  These tools provide concise, accessible information for quick reference during development. They help reinforce learning by summarizing key commands, processes, and best practices in a structured format.

- **Practical Exercises for Each Chapter:**
  Hands-on projects and exercises enable learners to apply theoretical concepts in real-world scenarios. They are designed with clear objectives, detailed instructions, starter code, and reflection questions to foster active learning and skill development.

By integrating these interactive tools and exercises into the learning process, students and practitioners can enhance their understanding, develop practical skills, and build confidence in applying agentic AI concepts to real-world projects.

12.3. Group Projects and Community Engagement

Overview

Group projects and community engagement are vital for advancing knowledge and skills in agentic AI. Collaborative projects not only enhance learning but also foster innovation by bringing together diverse perspectives. By working in teams, individuals can leverage each other's strengths, share expertise, and solve complex problems that might be challenging to tackle alone.

Importance of Collaborative Projects

- **Enhanced Learning:**
  Collaborative projects encourage active learning and practical application of theoretical concepts. Working in a group allows members to learn from each other's experiences and fill gaps in knowledge.
- **Diverse Perspectives:**
  Bringing together individuals from various backgrounds leads to creative problem-solving and innovative ideas. Different perspectives can lead to more comprehensive and robust AI solutions.
- **Networking Opportunities:**
  Engaging in group projects helps build professional networks, which can lead to future collaborations, mentorship, and career opportunities in the AI community.
- **Real-World Experience:**
  Group projects simulate real-world work environments where teamwork, communication, and project management are essential. This experience is invaluable when transitioning from academic learning to industry roles.

Types of Group Projects

1. **Hackathons:**
   Intensive, short-term events where participants collaborate to develop innovative AI solutions. These events encourage rapid prototyping and creative thinking.
2. **Open-Source Contributions:**
   Collaborative projects hosted on platforms like GitHub where community members contribute to AI libraries, tools, or applications. This experience improves coding skills and familiarity with collaborative software development practices.
3. **Team Challenges and Competitions:**
   Competitions such as those on Kaggle or other data science platforms, where teams work together to solve real-world problems using AI techniques.
4. **Research Collaborations:**
   Joint projects that involve investigating new AI algorithms or applications, often leading to publications or presentations at conferences.

Best Practices for Successful Group Projects

- **Clear Objectives:**
  Define the project scope, goals, and deliverables at the outset to ensure everyone is aligned.
- **Defined Roles and Responsibilities:**
  Assign roles such as project manager, lead developer, data engineer, and documentation specialist to streamline the work process.
- **Effective Communication:**
  Use collaboration tools like Slack, Microsoft Teams, or Discord for real-time communication and project management tools like Trello or Asana to track progress.
- **Regular Meetings and Updates:**
  Schedule periodic check-ins to discuss progress, address challenges, and adjust plans as needed.
- **Documentation and Knowledge Sharing:**
  Maintain detailed documentation of project decisions, code, and data workflows to ensure continuity and ease future maintenance.

Example Table: Group Projects and Collaboration Tools

Project Type	Description	Collaboration Tools

Hackathons	Short-term, intensive projects focused on rapid innovation	Slack, GitHub, Zoom
Open-Source Contributions	Collaborative development on public repositories	GitHub, GitLab, Bitbucket
Team Competitions	Data science challenges with real-world datasets	Kaggle, Google Colab, Microsoft Teams
Research Collaborations	Joint academic or industry research projects	Overleaf, Slack, Microsoft Teams, GitHub

12.4. Online Resources and Further Learning

Overview

Continuous learning is critical in the fast-evolving field of agentic AI. Online resources provide a wealth of information, from fundamental tutorials to advanced research papers. Leveraging these resources helps learners stay current with the latest advancements, best practices, and emerging trends in AI.

Key Online Resources

1. **Massive Open Online Courses (MOOCs):**
   o **Platforms:** Coursera, edX, Udacity, and Fast.ai.
   o **Content:** Offer structured courses on machine learning, deep learning, and specialized AI topics.
2. **Documentation and Official Guides:**
   o **Platforms:** TensorFlow, PyTorch, and scikit-learn provide comprehensive documentation and tutorials.
   o **Content:** Step-by-step guides, API references, and best practices for using these frameworks.
3. **Online Communities and Forums:**

- **Platforms:** Stack Overflow, Reddit (r/MachineLearning, r/artificial), and specialized Slack channels.
- **Content:** Active discussions, troubleshooting tips, and shared experiences from practitioners.
4. **Research Publications and Blogs:**
    - **Platforms:** arXiv.org, Google Scholar, and Medium.
    - **Content:** Latest research papers, industry insights, and detailed articles on cutting-edge AI topics.
5. **Interactive Platforms:**
    - **Platforms:** Kaggle and GitHub.
    - **Content:** Hands-on competitions, datasets, and open-source projects that offer practical experience.

Table: Online Resources for Agentic AI Learning

Resource Type	Platform/Website	Content/Benefits
MOOCs	Coursera, edX, Udacity	Structured courses on AI, machine learning, and deep learning
Framework Documentation	TensorFlow, PyTorch	Detailed API documentation, tutorials, and code examples
Online Communities	Stack Overflow, Reddit	Q&A forums for troubleshooting, discussion of best practices
Research Publications	arXiv.org, Google Scholar	Access to the latest research papers and academic publications
Interactive Platforms	Kaggle, GitHub	Hands-on projects, competitions, and

opportunities to contribute to open-source

Further Learning Paths

- **Specialization Programs:**
  Consider enrolling in specialized programs or nanodegrees that focus on advanced topics in agentic AI, such as reinforcement learning, computer vision, or natural language processing.
- **Conferences and Webinars:**
  Attend industry conferences (e.g., NeurIPS, ICML) and webinars to network with experts and learn about the latest research and trends.
- **Community Meetups:**
  Participate in local or virtual meetups and workshops to engage with the AI community, share experiences, and gain practical insights.
- **Personal Projects:**
  Build personal projects or contribute to open-source projects on GitHub to apply theoretical knowledge in real-world scenarios and improve your portfolio.

Example: Using GitHub API to Discover AI Projects

Below is a simple Python script that uses GitHub's API to search for popular agentic AI projects. This example demonstrates how to leverage online resources for further learning and exploration.

python

```python
import requests


def search_github_repositories(query, sort="stars", order="desc", per_page=5):
    """

    Search for GitHub repositories based on a query.

    Parameters:
```

```python
    query (str): Search term.

    sort (str): Sort parameter (e.g., stars, forks).

    order (str): Order (asc or desc).

    per_page (int): Number of results per page.
Returns:

    List of repository names and their URLs.
"""

url = "https://api.github.com/search/repositories"

params = {

    "q": query,

    "sort": sort,

    "order": order,

    "per_page": per_page

}

response = requests.get(url, params=params)

data = response.json()


repositories = []

for repo in data.get("items", []):

    repositories.append({

        "name": repo["name"],

        "url": repo["html_url"],

        "stars": repo["stargazers_count"]
```

```
        })

    return repositories


# Example usage:

if __name__ == "__main__":

    query = "agentic AI"

    repos = search_github_repositories(query)

    print("Top Agentic AI Repositories on GitHub:")

    for repo in repos:

        print(f"{repo['name']} ({repo['stars']} stars) - {repo['url']}")
```

Explanation:

- **Functionality:**
  The script uses GitHub's API to search for repositories related to "agentic AI", sorted by stars.
- **Parameters:**
  The function accepts parameters to customize the search, such as the number of results per page.
- **Output:**
  It prints out the top repositories along with their star counts and URLs, providing a gateway for further exploration.

Summary

- **Group Projects and Community Engagement:**
  Collaborative projects and community interactions enhance learning, foster innovation, and build networks. Clear objectives, defined roles, and effective communication tools are key to successful group projects.
- **Online Resources and Further Learning:**
  A wealth of online resources—MOOCs, official documentation, communities,

research publications, and interactive platforms—offer continuous learning opportunities. Leveraging these resources helps learners stay updated and deepen their expertise in agentic AI.

By integrating group projects, community engagement, and diverse online resources, learners can build practical skills, gain real-world experience, and continue advancing their knowledge in the ever-evolving field of agentic AI.

Chapter 13 The Future of Agentic AI

As we look ahead, agentic AI continues to evolve and expand its influence across various sectors. Ongoing research and technological advancements are setting the stage for a new era of intelligent systems—ones that are increasingly autonomous, adaptable, and capable of making complex decisions. In this section, we explore emerging trends and technological innovations that will shape the future of agentic AI, and we discuss the long-term vision of superintelligent autonomous systems.

13.1. Emerging Trends and Technological Innovations

Overview

The rapid pace of research and development in AI is fueling numerous trends and innovations. These advancements are driving the next generation of agentic AI, expanding its capabilities and applications. The following areas are expected to have significant impact in the coming years:

1. **Advances in Neural Architectures:**
   - **Deep Learning Evolution:**
     New architectures, such as transformers and graph neural networks, are pushing the boundaries of what neural networks can achieve. These models are designed to handle complex data structures and long-range dependencies more effectively than traditional deep learning models.
   - **Hybrid Models:**
     The integration of symbolic reasoning with neural networks aims to combine the best of both worlds—structured logic and data-driven learning.
2. **Reinforcement Learning (RL) Enhancements:**
   - **Continuous Learning:**
     Techniques that allow agents to learn continuously from their environment (lifelong learning) are under active development. This enables systems to adapt to changing conditions without needing complete retraining.
   - **Multi-Agent Reinforcement Learning:**
     The development of algorithms where multiple agents interact and learn from each other can lead to more sophisticated and robust autonomous systems.
3. **Edge Computing and Decentralized AI:**

- Distributed Processing:
  With the proliferation of Internet of Things (IoT) devices and advancements in edge computing, AI processing can be decentralized. This reduces latency and enables real-time decision-making closer to the data source.
- **Federated Learning:**
  This approach allows AI models to be trained across decentralized devices while maintaining data privacy, making it ideal for applications in healthcare, finance, and smart cities.

4. **Explainability and Trustworthy AI:**
   - **Interpretable Models:**
     There is growing emphasis on developing AI systems that can explain their decisions in human-understandable terms. This enhances transparency and trust, which are crucial for adoption in sensitive applications such as healthcare and legal systems.
   - **Ethical and Responsible AI Frameworks:**
     Organizations are increasingly adopting ethical guidelines and frameworks to ensure that AI systems are developed and deployed in a fair and responsible manner.

5. **Integration of AI with Emerging Technologies:**
   - **Quantum Computing:**
     While still in early stages, quantum computing promises to revolutionize AI by solving complex optimization and simulation problems much faster than classical computers.
   - **5G and Beyond:**
     The deployment of high-speed networks will facilitate real-time data processing and the seamless integration of AI into everyday devices.

Table: Emerging Trends in Agentic AI

Trend/Innovation	Description	Impact on Agentic AI
Advances in Neural Architectures	New models like transformers and hybrid symbolic-neural systems	Enhanced ability to process complex data and perform reasoning tasks

Reinforcement Learning Enhancements	Continuous and multi-agent learning strategies	More adaptive and robust autonomous systems
Edge Computing and Decentralization	AI processing at the network edge and federated learning	Reduced latency and improved data privacy
Explainable and Trustworthy AI	Development of interpretable models and ethical frameworks	Increased transparency and user trust, particularly in sensitive sectors
Integration with Emerging Technologies	Incorporating quantum computing and advanced network technologies	Potential breakthroughs in processing speed and capability

Example: Simulating a Federated Learning Scenario

While a complete federated learning implementation is complex, the following code snippet provides a basic simulation framework using Python. This example demonstrates how multiple clients might update a shared model without centralizing their data.

python

```python
import numpy as np


# Simulated global model parameters (for simplicity, a single weight)

global_model = np.array([0.5])


# Simulate local data on 3 different clients
```

```python
local_data = [np.random.rand(10) for _ in range(3)]

local_labels = [np.random.rand(10) for _ in range(3)]


def local_update(model, data, labels, lr=0.01):
    """

    Simulate a local update on client data.

    For demonstration, a dummy update is performed by subtracting the
    mean difference.

    """

    # Compute a simple gradient (dummy calculation)

    gradient = np.mean(data - labels)

    updated_model = model - lr * gradient

    return updated_model


# Each client updates the model locally
local_models = []
for data, labels in zip(local_data, local_labels):

    updated_model = local_update(global_model, data, labels)

    local_models.append(updated_model)

    print("Local updated model:", updated_model)


# Aggregation: Average the local model updates to form the new global
model

global_model = np.mean(local_models, axis=0)
```

```
print("\nAggregated Global Model:", global_model)
```

Explanation:

- **Global Model:**
  A simple model represented by a single weight is initialized.
- **Local Update:**
  Each client performs a dummy update based on its local data. In real federated learning, each client would train on its data and send updates to a central server.
- **Aggregation:**
  The central server aggregates local updates (here, by averaging) to update the global model.
- **Outcome:**
  This simulation illustrates the basic idea of decentralized learning, which is a key trend in making AI scalable and privacy-preserving.

13.2. The Road to Superintelligent Autonomous Systems

Overview

The concept of superintelligent autonomous systems—often referred to as superintelligence—represents a long-term vision where AI systems surpass human intelligence across all domains. While we are still far from achieving superintelligence, understanding the potential roadmap and challenges involved is crucial for both researchers and policymakers.

Key Milestones on the Road to Superintelligence

1. **Narrow AI to General AI:**
   - **Narrow AI:**
     Systems that excel in specific tasks (e.g., image recognition, natural language processing) are already prevalent.
   - **Artificial General Intelligence (AGI):**
     The next major milestone is developing systems that possess human-like cognitive abilities, allowing them to perform any intellectual task that a human can.
   - **Superintelligence:**
     An AI that surpasses human intelligence in virtually every field, including creativity, problem-solving, and emotional intelligence.

214

2. **Advances in Learning and Adaptation:**
    - **Lifelong Learning:**
      Future AI systems must continuously learn and adapt throughout their operational lifetime without requiring frequent retraining.
    - **Meta-Learning:**
      Systems that can learn how to learn, optimizing their own learning processes, will be crucial for achieving superintelligence.
3. **Ethical and Safe AI Development:**
    - **Alignment and Control:**
      A critical challenge is ensuring that superintelligent systems are aligned with human values and can be controlled or guided safely.
    - **Robustness and Security:**
      Superintelligent systems must be designed to be robust against manipulation, errors, and malicious use.
4. **Infrastructure and Integration:**
    - **Scalable Computing:**
      Superintelligence will require unprecedented computational resources and energy-efficient architectures.
    - **Interdisciplinary Integration:**
      Combining insights from neuroscience, cognitive science, and philosophy with AI research will be essential to build systems that truly understand and mimic human cognition.

Challenges and Considerations

- **Technical Complexity:**
  The development of superintelligent systems involves overcoming numerous technical challenges, from model architecture to efficient learning algorithms.
- **Ethical Risks:**
  The potential societal impact of superintelligent AI necessitates robust ethical frameworks and governance models to prevent misuse.
- **Economic and Social Disruption:**
  As AI capabilities grow, there may be significant implications for employment, social structures, and global power dynamics.
- **Regulatory and Governance Issues:**
  Policymakers must work proactively to establish regulations and oversight mechanisms that keep pace with technological advancements.

Table: Roadmap to Superintelligent Autonomous Systems

Milestone	Description	Key Challenges
Narrow AI	Systems designed for specific tasks (currently prevalent).	Limited scope, task-specific performance.
Artificial General Intelligence	Systems with human-like cognitive abilities.	Achieving flexible, context-aware reasoning.
Superintelligence	AI that exceeds human intelligence across all domains.	Control, alignment, robustness, and ethical oversight.
Lifelong and Meta-Learning	Continuous learning systems that optimize their learning processes.	Managing computational resources and ensuring stability.
Infrastructure & Integration	Scalable, energy-efficient computing combined with interdisciplinary insights.	Building the necessary hardware and integrating diverse fields.

Example: Conceptual Framework for Lifelong Learning

While a complete implementation of lifelong learning is an active area of research, the following pseudocode outlines a conceptual framework where an AI system continuously updates its knowledge base over time.

python

```python
class LifelongLearningAgent:

    def __init__(self, initial_model):
```

```python
    self.model = initial_model
    self.knowledge_base = []  # Store past experiences


def learn(self, new_data):
    """
    Incorporate new data into the model.
    This function represents the continual learning process.
    """
    # Update model with new data (simplified example)
    self.model.update(new_data)
    self.knowledge_base.append(new_data)


def predict(self, input_data):
    """
    Generate predictions based on the updated model.
    """
    return self.model.predict(input_data)


def review_knowledge(self):
    """
    Periodically review and consolidate learned knowledge.
    """
    # Pseudocode: Consolidate knowledge base to improve model efficiency
```

```
        self.knowledge_base = self.consolidate(self.knowledge_base)


    def consolidate(self, data):
        """

        A placeholder for a method to consolidate and prune outdated
information.

        """

        # This function would implement algorithms for knowledge distillation
and consolidation.

        return data


# Example usage (conceptual):

# agent = LifelongLearningAgent(initial_model)

# while True:

#     new_data = collect_new_data()

#     agent.learn(new_data)

#     prediction = agent.predict(latest_input)

#     agent.review_knowledge()
```

Explanation:

- **LifelongLearningAgent Class:**
  This class represents an AI agent that continuously updates its model based on new data.
- **Learning Process:**
  The learn method updates the model and stores new data in the knowledge base.

- **Knowledge Review:**
  The review_knowledge method periodically consolidates the knowledge base to ensure the model remains efficient.
- **Conceptual Nature:**
  This pseudocode outlines the framework; actual implementations would require complex algorithms for continuous learning and knowledge consolidation.

Summary

- **Emerging Trends and Technological Innovations:**
  Advancements in neural architectures, reinforcement learning, edge computing, explainable AI, and the integration of emerging technologies are reshaping the landscape of agentic AI. These innovations enable more robust, adaptive, and transparent systems.
- **The Road to Superintelligent Autonomous Systems:**
  The journey from narrow AI to superintelligence involves achieving artificial general intelligence, developing lifelong learning capabilities, and ensuring that advanced systems are safe, ethical, and aligned with human values. While the technical and ethical challenges are significant, ongoing research and interdisciplinary collaboration are paving the way toward this ambitious goal.

Together, these developments indicate a future where agentic AI will not only perform routine tasks but will also engage in complex decision-making, creative problem-solving, and continuous adaptation, ultimately transforming industries and society at large.

13.3. Potential Risks and Mitigation Strategies

Overview

As agentic AI continues to advance and integrate deeper into society and business, it is crucial to recognize and address potential risks associated with its deployment. These risks can range from technical challenges and data issues to ethical, societal, and economic concerns. Mitigation strategies involve technical safeguards, robust governance frameworks, continuous monitoring, and proactive engagement with regulatory standards and stakeholders.

Key Risks

1. **Technical Risks:**

- **Model Failures:** Inaccurate predictions or unexpected behavior due to model overfitting, underfitting, or data drift.
- **System Integration Errors:** Faults occurring when integrating various AI components (sensors, data processing, decision-making, actuation) leading to communication failures or performance bottlenecks.
- **Scalability Issues:** Difficulties in handling increased data loads or computational demands, which can result in degraded performance or system outages.

2. **Data-Related Risks:**
   - **Data Quality and Bias:** Poor-quality, biased, or unrepresentative data can lead to skewed predictions and unfair outcomes.
   - **Privacy and Security:** Risks of data breaches, unauthorized access, or misuse of sensitive personal information.

3. **Ethical and Societal Risks:**
   - **Lack of Transparency:** Opaque "black-box" models that make it difficult to understand and justify decisions.
   - **Ethical Misalignment:** AI systems that do not align with human values or ethical principles, leading to potential harm or discrimination.
   - **Job Displacement:** Economic and social challenges related to workforce displacement due to automation.

4. **Regulatory and Governance Risks:**
   - **Non-Compliance:** Failure to adhere to data protection, privacy laws, or industry regulations can result in legal repercussions and loss of trust.
   - **Governance Failures:** Inadequate oversight or accountability mechanisms that fail to detect or address issues promptly.

Mitigation Strategies

To address these risks, a multi-layered approach is required:

1. **Robust Technical Measures:**
   - **Continuous Monitoring:** Implement real-time monitoring of AI system performance, including anomaly detection and performance metrics.
   - **Model Validation and Testing:** Use rigorous testing, cross-validation, and stress-testing to ensure model robustness and adaptability.
   - **Scalability Planning:** Employ modular architectures, load balancing, and cloud-based solutions to handle scaling demands efficiently.

2. **Data Management and Security:**
   - **Data Quality Assurance:** Implement processes for data cleaning, regular audits, and bias detection to ensure high-quality, representative datasets.

- o **Encryption and Access Controls:** Use strong encryption protocols and strict access controls to protect sensitive data.
- o **Privacy by Design:** Incorporate privacy-preserving techniques such as data anonymization, pseudonymization, and federated learning.

3. **Ethical and Transparent Practices:**
   - o **Explainable AI (XAI):** Develop models that provide interpretable outputs to foster trust and accountability.
   - o **Ethical Frameworks:** Establish internal ethics boards and adhere to industry guidelines (e.g., IEEE, EU guidelines) to ensure AI systems align with ethical standards.
   - o **Stakeholder Engagement:** Involve diverse stakeholders (users, experts, regulators) in the development process to address societal concerns and build consensus.

4. **Regulatory Compliance and Governance:**
   - o **Regular Audits and Reporting:** Conduct internal and external audits to ensure compliance with legal standards such as GDPR, CCPA, HIPAA, and PCI-DSS.
   - o **Clear Governance Structures:** Establish transparent governance models that define roles, responsibilities, and accountability for AI outcomes.
   - o **Proactive Policy Engagement:** Stay informed about evolving regulations and actively engage with policymakers to help shape future AI regulations.

Comparative Table: Risks and Mitigation Strategies

Risk Category	Potential Risk	Mitigation Strategy	Example/Tools
Technical	Model failures, integration errors	Continuous monitoring, rigorous testing, modular design	Prometheus, unit tests, microservices
Data-Related	Data quality issues, bias, privacy breaches	Data cleaning, bias audits, encryption, privacy by design	Pandas, data anonymization, AES encryption

Ethical/Societal	Lack of transparency, ethical misalignment	Explainable AI, ethical frameworks, stakeholder engagement	LIME, ethics committees, public forums
Regulatory/Governance	Non-compliance, governance failures	Regular audits, clear governance structures, proactive policy engagement	GDPR compliance tools, internal audits

Practical Example: Monitoring for Anomaly Detection

Below is a Python code example using a simple moving average to detect anomalies in sensor data—an essential technique for monitoring technical performance.

python

```python
import numpy as np

import matplotlib.pyplot as plt


# Simulated sensor data (e.g., temperature readings)

data = np.random.normal(loc=25, scale=1, size=100)

# Introduce an anomaly

data[50:55] += 5  # Simulated spike


# Calculate moving average (window size 5)

window_size = 5
```

```python
moving_avg = np.convolve(data, np.ones(window_size)/window_size,
mode='valid')


# Simple anomaly detection: Flag readings that deviate from moving
average by > 2 standard deviations

threshold = 2 * np.std(data)

anomalies = []

for i in range(len(moving_avg)):

    if abs(data[i + window_size - 1] - moving_avg[i]) > threshold:

        anomalies.append(i + window_size - 1)


plt.figure(figsize=(10, 5))

plt.plot(data, label='Sensor Data', marker='o')

plt.plot(np.arange(window_size - 1, len(data)), moving_avg, label='Moving
Average', linestyle='--')

plt.scatter(anomalies, data[anomalies], color='red', label='Anomalies')

plt.title("Anomaly Detection in Sensor Data")

plt.xlabel("Time")

plt.ylabel("Sensor Reading")

plt.legend()

plt.show()
```

Explanation:

- **Data Simulation:**
  Generates simulated sensor data with a known anomaly.

223

- **Moving Average:**
  Computes a moving average to smooth the data and establish a baseline.
- **Anomaly Detection:**
  Flags data points that deviate significantly from the moving average.
- **Visualization:**
  Plots the data, moving average, and identified anomalies to help diagnose potential issues.

13.4. Preparing for an AI-Driven Future: Learning Outcomes

Overview

Preparing for an AI-driven future involves not only understanding the technology but also developing the skills, mindset, and strategies to navigate an increasingly AI-integrated world. The learning outcomes in this section focus on equipping individuals and organizations with the knowledge to leverage AI, address its challenges, and drive innovation responsibly.

Key Learning Outcomes

1. **Understanding Emerging Technologies:**
   - **Outcome:**
     Gain a comprehensive understanding of the latest advancements in neural architectures, reinforcement learning, edge computing, and explainable AI.
   - **Benefits:**
     Stay abreast of trends and be better prepared to adopt new technologies as they emerge.
2. **Risk Management and Ethical Oversight:**
   - **Outcome:**
     Develop the ability to identify potential risks, apply mitigation strategies, and integrate ethical considerations into AI development.
   - **Benefits:**
     Build trust, ensure compliance with regulatory frameworks, and promote responsible innovation.
3. **Scalability and System Maintenance:**
   - **Outcome:**
     Learn best practices for designing scalable AI systems, including modular architectures, load balancing, and efficient data management.

- **Benefits:**
  Ensure long-term system reliability, performance, and cost-effectiveness.

4. **Integration of Human and Machine Intelligence:**
   - **Outcome:**
     Understand how to blend human judgment with AI analytics to enhance decision-making and drive strategic outcomes.
   - **Benefits:**
     Achieve more nuanced and context-aware decisions that leverage the strengths of both humans and machines.

5. **Practical Implementation and Hands-On Experience:**
   - **Outcome:**
     Develop practical skills through interactive exercises, group projects, and real-world case studies.
   - **Benefits:**
     Gain confidence in applying theoretical concepts to tangible projects, fostering continuous learning and innovation.

Summary Table: Learning Outcomes for an AI-Driven Future

Learning Outcome	Description	Benefit
Understanding Emerging Technologies	Stay updated on latest AI innovations and trends.	Better technology adoption and competitive advantage.
Risk Management and Ethical Oversight	Identify, mitigate, and manage AI-related risks, including ethical challenges.	Improved trust, compliance, and responsible AI deployment.
Scalability and Maintenance	Design scalable systems and implement effective maintenance practices.	Reliable, efficient, and cost-effective AI systems.

Integration of Human and AI Intelligence	Combine AI-driven analytics with human judgment to enhance decision-making.	More robust and contextually aware strategic decisions.
Practical Implementation and Hands-On Experience	Apply concepts through interactive projects, exercises, and real-world case studies.	Enhanced practical skills and readiness for industry challenges.

Preparing for an AI-driven future means developing a balanced perspective that encompasses both technical mastery and ethical responsibility. By achieving these learning outcomes, individuals and organizations will be well-equipped to harness the transformative power of agentic AI while mitigating its risks. This comprehensive preparation will lead to more innovative, scalable, and ethically sound applications, driving sustainable progress in a rapidly changing world.

Chapter 14 Conclusion and Next Steps

In this final section, we summarize the essential concepts, strategies, and practical applications discussed throughout the book on agentic AI. We then explore advanced topics and outline future learning paths to help you continue developing your expertise in this rapidly evolving field.

14.1. Recap of Key Learnings and Insights

Overview

Throughout this book, we have delved into the fundamental principles, technical underpinnings, and practical applications of agentic AI. The key learnings span from understanding basic definitions to implementing autonomous systems and integrating AI with human decision-making. Below is a comprehensive recap of these insights.

Key Concepts Recap

- **Foundations of Agentic AI:**
    - **Definitions and Terminology:** Understanding essential terms such as autonomy, perception, decision-making, actuation, and adaptability.
    - **Core Components:** The building blocks include sensor data processing, model training, feedback loops, and adaptive learning mechanisms.
- **Technical Mechanics:**
    - **Algorithms Driving Autonomy:** A combination of rule-based and learning-based algorithms underpin the decision-making processes of autonomous agents.
    - **Neural Networks and Reinforcement Learning:** These techniques enable agents to learn from data and improve performance over time.
- **Data as the Fuel for AI:**
    - **Data Collection and Preprocessing:** Emphasis on gathering high-quality, diverse datasets and applying rigorous cleaning and feature engineering processes.
    - **Model Training and Evaluation:** Methods for training, validating, and fine-tuning AI models to ensure accuracy and generalization.
- **Development and Implementation:**
    - **Setting Up the Environment:** Importance of a well-configured development environment, use of virtual environments, and selecting the right tools (e.g., TensorFlow, PyTorch).

- **Building Autonomous Agents:** Step-by-step guides and hands-on projects that illustrate the practical implementation of agentic AI systems.
- **Practical Applications and Industry Impact:**
  - **Business and Consumer Applications:** Case studies and simulations demonstrate how agentic AI transforms operations, marketing, supply chain management, and customer engagement.
  - **Integration with Human Judgment:** Blending AI analytics with human expertise for improved decision-making and strategic planning.
- **Ethical, Privacy, and Governance Considerations:**
  - **Ethics and Bias Mitigation:** Strategies to ensure fairness, transparency, and accountability in AI systems.
  - **Regulatory Compliance:** Overview of privacy laws, data protection measures, and governance models to ensure responsible AI deployment.
- **Scalability, Maintenance, and Troubleshooting:**
  - **Optimizing Performance:** Best practices for scalable architectures, continuous monitoring, and maintenance routines to keep AI systems robust and efficient.

Recap Table: Key Learnings Overview

Topic	Key Learnings	Impact
Foundations of Agentic AI	Basic terminology, core components, and sensor-to-action workflows	Establishes a strong conceptual foundation
Technical Mechanics	Algorithms, neural networks, reinforcement learning	Enables autonomous decision-making and continuous improvement
Data Management	Importance of data quality, preprocessing, model training and evaluation	Directly influences model performance and reliability

Development Environment	Virtual environments, tool selection (TensorFlow, PyTorch)	Streamlines development and promotes reproducibility
Practical Applications	Case studies, simulations, and real-world implementations	Demonstrates transformative impact on business and consumers
Ethical and Regulatory Considerations	Ensuring fairness, privacy, transparency, and adherence to regulations	Builds trust and facilitates responsible innovation
Scalability and Maintenance	Best practices for architecture, monitoring, and troubleshooting	Ensures long-term system efficiency and robustness

Code Example: Summary Script

The following simple Python script serves as a "digital summary" that prints out the key topics and insights, reinforcing the learning outcomes discussed above.

python

```python
def print_summary():

  summary = {

    "Foundations": "Understand key AI concepts: autonomy, perception, decision-making, actuation.",

    "Technical Mechanics": "Learn algorithms, neural networks, and reinforcement learning for autonomous systems.",

    "Data Management": "Collect, preprocess, and ensure high-quality data to fuel AI models.",
```

```
    "Development Environment": "Set up virtual environments and select
tools like TensorFlow and PyTorch.",

    "Practical Applications": "Apply agentic AI in business, marketing,
supply chain, and customer service.",

    "Ethical & Regulatory": "Integrate ethical guidelines, ensure privacy,
and comply with legal standards.",

    "Scalability & Maintenance": "Optimize system performance through
modular design, monitoring, and regular updates."

    }


    print("Key Learnings Recap:")

    for topic, insight in summary.items():

        print(f"- {topic}: {insight}")


if __name__ == "__main__":

    print_summary()
```

Explanation:

- The script defines a function that prints out a dictionary of key learnings, reinforcing the major points covered in the book.
- This simple digital summary can serve as a quick review tool for learners.

14.2. Advanced Topics and Future Learning Paths

Overview

While this book provides a comprehensive foundation in agentic AI, the field is rapidly evolving. Advanced topics and further learning paths offer opportunities to dive deeper into specialized areas, explore cutting-edge research, and acquire skills that will be essential for future innovations. This section outlines advanced subjects and suggests resources for continuous learning.

Advanced Topics for Further Exploration

1. **Artificial General Intelligence (AGI) and Superintelligence:**
   o **Description:**
     Explore the theoretical and practical aspects of AGI, systems that possess human-level cognitive abilities, and the eventual possibility of superintelligent AI.
   o **Focus Areas:**
     - Cognitive architectures and meta-learning.
     - Ethical implications and control mechanisms for superintelligent systems.

2. **Advanced Reinforcement Learning:**
   o **Description:**
     Delve into complex RL techniques, such as multi-agent reinforcement learning, hierarchical RL, and continuous learning strategies.
   o **Focus Areas:**
     - Policy optimization methods.
     - Real-world applications in robotics, autonomous vehicles, and strategic games.

3. **Explainable and Transparent AI:**
   o **Description:**
     Investigate techniques to improve AI transparency and accountability. This includes developing models that offer interpretable outputs and understanding the underlying decision processes.
   o **Focus Areas:**
     - Explainable AI (XAI) frameworks.
     - User-centric model evaluation and transparency metrics.

4. **Quantum Computing and AI:**
   o **Description:**
     Study the intersection of quantum computing and AI, exploring how quantum algorithms could revolutionize optimization and learning.
   o **Focus Areas:**
     - Quantum machine learning algorithms.
     - Practical challenges in implementing quantum-enhanced AI.

5. **Advanced Data Science and Big Data Analytics:**
   o **Description:**
     Enhance your skills in handling and analyzing massive datasets, using

advanced statistical methods, and leveraging distributed computing frameworks.

- ○ **Focus Areas:**
  - Deep learning for unstructured data.
  - Real-time analytics using frameworks like Apache Spark and Flink.

Future Learning Paths and Resources

- **MOOCs and Online Courses:**
  - ○ Enroll in advanced courses on platforms like Coursera, edX, Udacity, or Fast.ai that focus on deep learning, reinforcement learning, and AI ethics.
  - ○ Recommended courses: "Deep Learning Specialization" by Andrew Ng, "Advanced Machine Learning" on Coursera, "Reinforcement Learning" by David Silver.
- **Research Papers and Journals:**
  - ○ Regularly read research publications from arXiv, IEEE, and ACM to stay updated on the latest advancements.
  - ○ Participate in academic conferences such as NeurIPS, ICML, and CVPR.
- **Professional Certifications and Nanodegrees:**
  - ○ Consider pursuing certifications or nanodegree programs that offer in-depth training in AI and machine learning.
  - ○ Programs such as the TensorFlow Developer Certificate or Udacity's AI Nanodegree can provide structured learning paths.
- **Community and Networking:**
  - ○ Join AI research groups, local meetups, or online forums (e.g., Reddit, LinkedIn groups) to network with peers and experts.
  - ○ Engage in hackathons, Kaggle competitions, or open-source projects to apply advanced concepts in real-world settings.
- **Books and Publications:**
  - ○ Continue reading advanced texts on AI, such as "Deep Learning" by Ian Goodfellow, Yoshua Bengio, and Aaron Courville, or "Reinforcement Learning: An Introduction" by Sutton and Barto.

Table: Advanced Topics and Learning Resources

Advanced Topic	Key Focus Areas	Suggested Resources

Artificial General Intelligence	Cognitive architectures, meta-learning, ethical implications	Research papers, NeurIPS proceedings, specialized workshops
Advanced Reinforcement Learning	Multi-agent systems, hierarchical RL, policy optimization	Coursera's Advanced RL courses, David Silver's lectures
Explainable and Transparent AI	XAI frameworks, interpretability techniques	Tutorials on LIME, SHAP; IEEE publications on explainability
Quantum Computing and AI	Quantum algorithms for machine learning, computational challenges	IBM Quantum Experience, research articles on quantum ML
Advanced Data Science & Big Data	Distributed computing, real-time analytics, deep learning for unstructured data	Apache Spark courses, online MOOCs on big data analytics

Reflection and Next Steps

- **Self-Assessment:**
  Reflect on the concepts covered in this book. Identify areas where you feel confident and topics that require further exploration.
- **Project-Based Learning:**
  Apply advanced topics to personal or group projects. Experiment with different frameworks and techniques to solidify your understanding.
- **Continuous Learning:**
  Develop a structured learning plan that includes online courses, reading research papers, participating in competitions, and joining community discussions.

Summary

- **Recap of Key Learnings:**
  The book has provided a comprehensive overview of agentic AI—from foundational principles and technical mechanics to practical applications and ethical considerations. The key learnings span data management, system design, human-AI integration, and robust governance.
- **Advanced Topics and Future Paths:**
  Looking forward, emerging areas such as AGI, advanced reinforcement learning, explainable AI, quantum computing, and big data analytics offer exciting avenues for further exploration. By engaging with advanced courses, research publications, professional certifications, and community activities, you can continue to evolve your expertise and remain at the forefront of AI innovation.

14.3. Final Thoughts on the Evolution of Agentic AI

The journey of agentic AI from early theoretical concepts to today's advanced autonomous systems has been marked by continuous innovation, adaptation, and interdisciplinary collaboration. Over the years, several key milestones have defined its evolution:

- **Foundational Beginnings:**
  Early work in artificial intelligence focused on rule-based systems and symbolic reasoning. Pioneers like Alan Turing and early expert systems laid the groundwork for thinking about machines that could mimic human cognition.
- **Transition to Learning-Based Models:**
  The advent of machine learning revolutionized the field. With the rise of neural networks and deep learning, AI systems moved from static, pre-programmed behavior to dynamic models capable of learning from vast amounts of data.
- **Emergence of Autonomous Systems:**
  Agentic AI represents the culmination of these advancements. By integrating sophisticated algorithms, reinforcement learning, and real-time data processing, modern autonomous agents can perceive their environment, make informed decisions, and adapt continuously.
- **Integration with Human Expertise:**
  Today's AI systems are increasingly designed to augment human decision-making rather than replace it. This hybrid approach, blending machine efficiency with human intuition, is key to navigating complex, real-world challenges.
- **Ethical and Regulatory Maturation:**
  As agentic AI evolves, so does the emphasis on ethics, transparency, and accountability. The development of frameworks for explainable AI, bias

mitigation, and data protection ensures that the progress in technology aligns with societal values and legal standards.

Reflective Summary

In summary, the evolution of agentic AI is characterized by:

- **Technological Breakthroughs:** Continuous advancements in algorithms, hardware, and data science.
- **Interdisciplinary Synergy:** Integration of insights from neuroscience, cognitive science, and ethics.
- **Practical Impact:** Broad applications ranging from autonomous vehicles to intelligent business systems.
- **Responsible Innovation:** A growing commitment to ensure that AI benefits society while minimizing risks.

Table: Evolution Milestones in Agentic AI

Stage	Key Innovations	Impact
Early AI	Rule-based systems, symbolic reasoning	Laid the foundational theories of machine intelligence.
Machine Learning Era	Statistical learning, neural networks	Introduced dynamic, data-driven decision-making.
Deep Learning Revolution	Deep neural networks, reinforcement learning	Enabled high-performance, adaptive autonomous systems.
Modern Agentic AI	Integration with human judgment, ethical frameworks	Enhanced real-world applicability with a focus on responsible innovation.

These milestones highlight the transformative progress in AI over the decades and provide a roadmap for future advancements.

14.4. Staying Updated in a Rapidly Changing Field

In the fast-paced world of AI, continuous learning and staying informed are critical. The field evolves rapidly, with new breakthroughs, techniques, and ethical challenges emerging regularly. Here are some strategies and resources to help you remain current.

Strategies for Staying Updated

1. **Engage in Continuous Learning:**
   - **Online Courses and MOOCs:**
     Enroll in advanced courses on platforms such as Coursera, edX, Udacity, and Fast.ai. These courses are frequently updated to reflect the latest research.
   - **Certifications and Nanodegrees:**
     Consider pursuing certifications (e.g., TensorFlow Developer Certificate) or nanodegree programs to gain structured, in-depth knowledge.
2. **Follow Research Publications and Conferences:**
   - **Research Papers:**
     Regularly read preprints on arXiv.org and journals like IEEE Transactions on Neural Networks, and ACM Computing Surveys.
   - **Conferences:**
     Attend or follow major conferences such as NeurIPS, ICML, CVPR, and AAAI to learn about cutting-edge research and network with experts.
3. **Participate in Online Communities:**
   - **Forums and Social Media:**
     Join discussion groups on Reddit (e.g., r/MachineLearning, r/artificial), LinkedIn, and specialized AI forums.
   - **GitHub and Open-Source Projects:**
     Contribute to or follow open-source projects to see practical implementations and code updates.
4. **Subscribe to Newsletters and Blogs:**
   - **Newsletters:**
     Subscribe to newsletters like "Import AI," "The Batch" by Andrew Ng, or "AI Weekly" for curated updates.

- ○ **Blogs and Podcasts:**
  Follow influential blogs and listen to podcasts from leaders in the field to gain insights into emerging trends and industry perspectives.
5. **Attend Webinars and Workshops:**
   - ○ **Virtual Events:**
     Many organizations offer webinars and workshops that cover recent advancements, ethical considerations, and practical applications.
   - ○ **Local Meetups:**
     Participate in local AI meetups or hackathons to engage with the community and gain hands-on experience.

Tools and Resources for Continuous Learning

Resource Type	Examples	Benefits
Online Courses/Certifications	Coursera, edX, Udacity, Fast.ai	Structured learning, updated content, and certification value
Research Publications	arXiv, IEEE Xplore, Google Scholar	Access to the latest academic and applied research findings
Conferences/Webinars	NeurIPS, ICML, CVPR, AAAI, MIT Technology Review Webinars	Networking, exposure to cutting-edge ideas, and professional growth
Online Communities	Reddit (r/MachineLearning, r/artificial), GitHub, Stack Overflow	Collaborative learning, troubleshooting, and community support

| Newsletters/Blogs | Import AI, The Batch, AI Weekly, Towards Data Science | Curated updates, industry insights, and diverse perspectives |

Example: Automating Updates with RSS Feeds

You can automate the process of staying updated by using RSS feeds to collect the latest news from your favorite AI blogs and journals. Here is a simple Python script that uses the feedparser library to fetch and display the latest headlines from an AI research feed.

python

```python
import feedparser


def fetch_latest_news(feed_url):
    """

    Fetch and display the latest news headlines from an RSS feed.


    Parameters:

        feed_url (str): The URL of the RSS feed.


    Returns:

        None
    """

    feed = feedparser.parse(feed_url)

    print("Latest News Headlines:")

    for entry in feed.entries[:5]:
```

```python
    print(f"- {entry.title}")

    print(f"  Link: {entry.link}\n")


if __name__ == "__main__":

    # Example RSS feed for AI research (adjust URL as needed)

    ai_feed_url = "http://export.arxiv.org/rss/cs.AI"

    fetch_latest_news(ai_feed_url)
```

Explanation:

- **Feedparser Library:**
  The script uses the feedparser library to parse an RSS feed.
- **Fetching Latest News:**
  It retrieves the latest entries from an AI research feed (e.g., arXiv's AI category) and prints the top five headlines along with links.
- **Outcome:**
  This tool can be integrated into your regular routine to quickly scan the latest developments in AI.

The evolution of agentic AI has been a transformative journey marked by significant technological advancements, interdisciplinary collaboration, and increasing integration with ethical and governance frameworks. As you reflect on these final thoughts and prepare for an AI-driven future, it is crucial to embrace continuous learning and community engagement. By leveraging diverse resources and staying active in the field, you can remain at the forefront of innovation and contribute to the responsible advancement of AI technologies.